Jen,
May the Lord
Bless you always,
Cathy Farr

# I Am a Dirt Sandwich

Catherine J. Bowen

WESTBOW·
PRESS
A DIVISION OF THOMAS NELSON
& ZONDERVAN

# DEDICATION

This book is dedicated to the memory of Sandra Kay (Dembinski) Hayden (1950 - 2005), who led me to give my life to the Lord on March 15, 1979. Without her love and persistence, I would not have survived to March 16. I am still thankful every day for her friendship.

# ACKNOWLEDGEMENTS

Thank you to my dear friends, David and Charlene Glore, for the design of the artwork I used in this book and for their constant encouragement.

Also, a heartfelt thanks to my friend, Linda Coon, who diligently proofed and edited my manuscript. Her skills and talents are greatly appreciated.

And, special thanks to my husband, Bob, who fixed my technical problems and offered me patience and love when I wanted to give up.

# CONTENTS

# PREFACE

Rushing Waters: A Ministry

This compilation of the messages I created over the past 5 years is an opportunity to show how an ordinary wife, mother and grandmother can use life's experiences to further the kingdom of God. My ministry started out just sending encouragement to a few of my friends and grew over time through their sharing with others, and those extended friends sharing with their friends. I honestly don't know how many people read my messages each week. I leave that detail to the Lord.

The name, Rushing Waters, is taken from Ezekiel 43:2: *and I saw the glory of the God of Israel coming from the east. His voice was like the roar of rushing waters, and the land was radiant with his glory.* (New International Version) My purpose for this ministry is simple: to give glory to God and his Son, Jesus Christ.

I write because I have to. I have always seen the world from the perspective of how the events around me would look in print. From the neighborhood newspaper I started when I was 9 to this book, I have recorded – either in my head – or on paper my views of life, love and hope.

I have tried to live according to God's Word. Of course, the operative word is "tried" because I have neither succeeded all the time nor failed all the time.

My hope is that you will relate to my experiences and find yourself loving God, the life he has given you and striving for the perfection that will be complete in the day of Jesus Christ.

# INTRODUCTION

I have arranged the messages in the following categories:

- Faith
- Love
- Prayer
- Hope
- Joy
- Peace

These words represent the core of the Christian heart to me. If we can find joy, hope and peace through faith, love and prayer, we are livin' the dream.

Please take these messages in the spirit they were written – with a heart for the Lord and a life lived beyond anything I could have done on my own.

*For I know the plans I have for you," declares the LORD, "plans to prosper you and not to harm you, plans to give you hope and a future."* (Jeremiah 29:11)

All Bible references are taken from the New International Version, copyright ©1978 by the New York International Bible Society, used by permission of Zondervan Bible Publishers, unless otherwise noted.

King James Version references are taken from www.biblegateway. com as well as from my memory of verses I learned over the years.

I Am a Dirt Sandwich

*For I know that good itself does not dwell in me, that is, in my sinful nature. For I have the desire to do what is good, but I cannot carry it out.* (Romans 7:18)

Do you remember making dirt sandwiches in your sandbox as a kid? We used all sorts of things to put the dirt between: hankies, doll clothes, and real white bread if we could sneak it out of the house. We never actually ate them, but they were fun to pretend with at our tea parties. It got me to thinking how the core of that sandwich is a lot like us when we keep sinning after we have received Christ as Savior. We cover our outsides with the forgiveness we receive and continue to blacken the core of our hearts with sin.

There are too many times in my life when I could have chosen a better way; I could have done the right thing; I could have offered the gift of salvation. But I didn't. I either wanted something for myself so badly that I ignored the more righteous path, or, in the case of offering the gift of salvation, I just plain chickened out.

I am a dirt sandwich.

How can I keep asking the Lord to cleanse me when I know in my heart I am going to sin again? It seems pointless. But Paul answers that very question in Romans 7: 19 – 25. Simply, God continues to forgive us because we belong to him. While the war of sin vs good wages within us, we come through still belonging to Christ and living under his infinite grace.

So, should we just continue to sin knowing that we will be forgiven? No! Because we will miss the good things awaiting those who are obedient and living within God's will. He loves us so much that he gives the power to conquer our sinful natures if we read his Word, pray for his guidance and surrender our wills to his.

We can be clean clear through. We can ditch the dirt and know that Christ reigns in us to cleanse, heal and build a new, more sin-resistant nature.

Praise be to God!

Prayer: Please cleanse me, Lord. I am waiting upon you. Amen.

This Old House

*Don't you know that you yourselves are God's temple and that God's Spirit lives in you? Do you not know that your bodies are temples of the Holy Spirit, who is in you, whom you have received from God? You are not your own; you were bought at a price. Therefore, honor God with your body.* (1Corinthians 3:16, 6:19 – 20)

Do you ever have one of those days when you just can't get your motor going? It seems like every step you take causes pain somewhere. Of course I'm speaking to my older friends here, but you young ones can view it as something to look forward to. Some days I think if my body is a temple, the walls must be crumbling and the foundation is sinking. I'm like an episode of "This Old House." I used to amaze my sister that I could lie flat on the floor and do sit ups, no bent knees… and I was in my early fifties. Now I'm lucky to get down on the floor at all, and forget about getting up. Without help, I'm a beached whale.

It seems that even though I want to care for the temple God has placed in me through his Holy Spirit, I am losing any gains as fast as I make them. At least I try to be careful with what I put in my body. I limit alcohol, foods that are bad for me, medicines.

But I also try to be careful with what I think and read as well. I ask the Lord to give me the discernment to sort through the boatload of information I take in each day to sift out the useless and harmful and to keep the good - not easy in this era of technological downloads – at our fingertips 24/7.

The good news is that my thoughts and actions aren't necessarily dependent upon my physical well- being. Yes, I am a temple of God, but it's more in the sense that I think and act in ways that are spiritually positive than just physical attributes. "Take every thought captive," says Paul to the Corinthians. "And make it obedient to Christ."

**Every thought, every action is either an insult or a praise to our heavenly Father.** We are caught up in the game of sin, or we are fighting to stay on the winning side. I admit it isn't easy, and it probably never will be. But, we can fix up our rundown "temples" through:

- Prayer
- Fasting
- Giving
- Serving
- Devouring God's Word

Remodel if you have to. Tear down and start over if necessary. Just don't live in a broken-down, sinful shell – not when there is a mansion waiting for you.

Prayer: Lord, bless this temple you have built in me. I want to be the best I can be for you. Amen.

Five Smooth Stones

*Now the Israelites had been saying, "Do you see how this man keeps coming out? He comes out to defy Israel. The king will give great wealth to the man who kills him. He will also give him his daughter in marriage and will exempt his family from taxes in Israel." [26] David asked the men standing near him, "What will be done for the man who kills this Philistine and removes this disgrace from Israel? Who is this uncircumcised Philistine that he should defy the armies of the living God?"* (1Samuel 17: 24 – 26)

We're all familiar with the story of David and Goliath and how David slew the giant with his slingshot. Some key points stand out for me.

First, Saul who was king at the time of the Philistine invasion, was basically hiding from the enemy. He had lost his faith that God would protect him, but David was full of admiration and respect for the God of Israel. He told Saul that the same God who had rescued him from the bears and lions in the fields where he was shepherding his sheep would rescue him from this Philistine. David was frankly appalled at the cowardice of the king of Judah; he simply didn't understand why Saul would allow an enemy to defile the sacred ground where God had placed them.

And so, after rejecting the clothing and armor that Saul offered, David went out and chose five smooth stones with which to slay Goliath. Just five smooth stones and a slingshot. The kid had guts; you have to give him that. But the stones were just the weapons he held in his hands. The real weapon was his love for God and his willingness to lay it all on the line to save his people. He was offended for God. Without a second thought, David let it be known that he would go against the Philistine, the sworn enemy of Israel. Would any of <u>us</u> be so eager to serve God? Would any of <u>us</u> lay it all (our very lives) on the line for our God?

We may find ourselves in that situation someday. We have become over-confident in the freedoms we enjoy – the "unalienable rights" to life, liberty and the pursuit of happiness which we as Americans consider to be endowed by our Creator. But we must never forget the primary right we receive when we surrender our lives to Jesus Christ:

"Yet to all who received him, to all who believed in his name, he gave the right to become the children of God." (John 1:12). And we may be called upon to defend that right to man but never to God himself. And we will need more than a slingshot.

Consider those five smooth stones as prayers. They are the weapons you can use to slay your enemies – fear, jealousy, selfishness, anger, unbelief. I don't think any of us will face a "Goliath" as far as pure stature is concerned. But we will face the giants of our own making, and we can only triumph over them with the help of our Lord.

Prayer: Lord remind me to put on the full armor of God to find strength and power. Amen.

The Opposite of Selfishness

*Incline my heart to your testimonies, and not to selfish gain!* (Psalm 119:36)

What do you think the opposite of selfishness is? Selflessness? Humility? Doormat? I think the opposite of selfishness is holiness. "'Be holy as I am holy,' says the Lord." (1Peter 1:16) This phrase is the embodiment of what God has called each of us to do. We don't have to piecemeal it into characteristics and address some while declaring another too difficult to achieve. We must strive to be holy in all ways.

Being holy means being set apart for God's purposes, not our own. If you belong to him, you are called to a life of obedience. This obedience leads us to self-denial, moral righteousness, service and truth. Your life of holiness is lived through Jesus, a free gift of God. Without Jesus' sacrifice, we could not possibly strive for holiness. It would be an impossible task ending in frustration and failure.

But we serve a risen Savior who exhorts us to strive for the perfection of holiness, and he promises to bring it to completion: "And I am sure that he who began this good work in you will bring it to completion in the day of Jesus Christ." (Philippians 1:6) We must also exhort one another, encourage each other, and remind each other of the task before us: "'Be holy as I am holy,' says the Lord." (1Peter 1: 16)

ᵒogle the word holy. It's an interesting exercise in how our culture ᵃches the word.

ᵗ it means in your life.

ᵗnt to be holy, your kind of holy. Help me each day ᵒu. Amen.

## A Triune God

*Come near to Me, listen to this: from the first I have not spoken in secret, from the time it took place, I was there, and now Adonai-Yehovah has sent Me and His Spirit.* (Isaiah 48:16)

I was driving yesterday with my granddaughter, Grace, when she started talking about what Jesus looks like. She said, "of course we don't really know what God looks like; well, except for that little boy who went up to heaven and came back down to tell us."

I reminded her that the little boy who wrote *Heaven is for Real* was describing Jesus, not God because no one has ever seen God. "But," she continued, "if Jesus is God, wouldn't they look the same?" Great question. I told her the images we have of Jesus are of his human life, not his life as part of the trinity. We can't see the triune God; we just know the trinity exists. She confessed that she finds it all very confusing.

Join the club, I thought. It is confusing. But, I also told her not to get too caught up in trying to understand or explain it. "Just accept it," I said. "God said it; we believe it; and that settles it."

We can picture God however we like: grandfatherly, a pillar of fire, a dark cloud, a burning bush. But the real power of God lies in our ability to accept his Sovereignty, his unchanging devotion to his people. We were blessed by the human presence of Jesus, and we are continually blessed by the help of the Holy Spirit. And while we struggle with the three-in-one concept, it is not insurmountable. I like to picture it as a pillar of fire with the image of Jesus emerging from the left, and the cloudy wind of the Holy Spirit emerging from the right. But you can conjure up your own image as long as it retains the truth of the trinity.

The trinity is often the idea that atheists challenge when attacking what they consider to be a ridiculous and impossible concept. They claim it doesn't make sense; these gods have to be separate and therefore, independent. You can't have one God; you have to say you have three Gods. No I don't. I serve a God who is the author of all things; He can do and be whatever he says. The problem is we want to fit everything into our human understanding, our world box so that we can pick it apart, re-invent it, and turn it into what suits us. We feel the need to reduce God to our level of interpretation and understanding, not rise to His level of love and grace.

You may have heard the saying, God created man in his own image, and man returned the favor. We can't fit God in a box of our own making. He is too big. We need to celebrate that truth, not fight it.

Read John 1: 1 – 18 and absorb the words that support the Trinity. God isn't trying to fool us or make it difficult to believe in him. He is telling us that he has us covered; he's got our backs and takes the very form we need at every turn: Creator, Savior, Helper.

What more could we need or want?

Prayer: Lord, thank you for your Son and your Holy Spirit. May I always turn to the trinity for peace and comfort. Amen.

A Place for Me

*His* (the man who fears the Lord) *heart is secure; he will have no fear; in the end he will look in triumph on his foes.* (Psalm 112:8)

In our old house I had a wicker chair in the kitchen. There was a small table next to it where I kept my current reading material (books, magazines, my Bible study materials), and I loved to sit in that chair in the middle of the chaos of the day and just read. That chair made me feel secure; I could sink down against its tall back and enjoy a few minutes of peace. It was MY place; no one else sat there – they didn't want to.

I wish I had such a place in my kitchen today. There are plenty of places to sit, but there is no one place that is just mine. For some reason it feels better to have that one place that is secure, uncomplicated, mine alone.

While I don't have a wicker chair to claim, I do have a secure, uncomplicated place to go. I can settle into the arms of the Lord any time I need to feel safe. He is the only one who can save me from my fears. The foes David describes in the book of Psalms were warrior enemies in some cases; in others they were his own family. But David knows his God will defeat all of those enemies. And I know he will defeat mine as well even though they aren't warriors in a battle. They are still real to me – loss, pain, unkindness, lack of respect from loved ones. But, remember, those of us who love Jesus have already overcome the world – and all that goes with it. He is greater than any enemy – real or imagined – that we claim.

Read again Romans 8: 28 – 39. God is never going to abandon his children; we are his, and he will bring us to victory at the time of his choosing.

Until then, look in triumph over your foes; have no fear.

Prayer: Our Lord, our hope! Thank you for overcoming the world. Amen.

Seventh Inning Stretch

*In my Father's house are many rooms; if it were not so, I would have told you. I am going there to prepare a place for you. And if I go and prepare a place for you, I will come back and take you to be with me that you also may be where I am.* (John 14:2 & 3)

"OK, Cub fans, let me hear ya!" Harry Carey started the seventh inning stretch at every home game with these words. Those of us who have followed the Cubs for an entire lifetime can still hear Harry continue with his rendition of "Take Me Out to the Ball Game". Since Harry's passing, the stretch has been sung by many well-known celebrities and some not so well known. It is always interesting to me how each one can hit that first note just right while others are so far off, they never get back in tune.

I see a great parallel between that seventh inning stretch and our own seventh inning of life. I estimate it's around age fifty-five to sixty. You still have some time, but if you are on the losing side, you need to buckle down and get some runs. You've missed a lot of opportunities, but there is still time to win the game. If you hit that first note right, you can count on getting the rest right, too.

And so it is with life. If you start on the right note with Christ as Savior, you are assured a victory. If you miss that note, you spend a great deal of time and energy trying to get back on track and never quite making it happen. Jesus has the winning team, and if you aren't on it, death will win the game.

But remember that Christ has conquered the grave, and all who believe in him have conquered it also. (Read 1Corinthians 15: 54 – 56)

It's time to review your own winning strategy: is your life on key or hopelessly out of tune? Is Christ your Savior, or are you still trying to make it on your own? Is the Lord preparing a place for you in heaven or hell? You are the only one who can determine your eternal future. Christ has done all he can: he gave his life on the cross.

Now, it's up to you. And, just to finish this seventh inning analogy – Let's get some runs!

Prayer: Lord, help me make the most of my own seventh inning. Give me courage to share my winning strategy with others. Amen.

True Grit

Scripture: *Greater love hath no man than this, that a man lay down his life for his friends. Ye are my friends, if ye do the things which I command you.* (John 15:13-14 (American Standard Version)

We recently saw the movie, "True Grit". If you saw the 1969 version, this one will be a bit of a shocker – much more violent and graphic. But John Wayne is no Jeff Bridges, and Glen Campbell is certainly no Matt Damon. In both versions, Rooster Cogburn, Texas Marshall, is hired by a young woman to avenge the death of her father by bringing in the man who shot him.

Rooster starts out to get what he wants (the reward) and ends up going to the brink of death to save his young employer. He learns just what he is made of, and he is more surprised than anyone at what he finds.

In the scripture taken from the fifteenth chapter of John's gospel, we learn that Jesus is getting ready to make this ultimate sacrifice for his friends. He doesn't just go to the brink of death, he succumbs to the will of his Father and gives up his life on the cross. We don't see this kind of sacrifice all that much today. There are a few examples: the man who covered his wife with his own body to protect her from the crazed shooter in Tucson; our friend's brother who covered his blind mother during a bank robbery in Quincy, IL several years ago. And, we would all certainly lay down our lives for our children.

Jesus willingly went through the suffering and dying by crucifixion to save all of his children. He knew each of his children, and he chose to sacrifice himself for his friends – you and me. I've been reading A. W. Tozer's book, *The Pursuit of God*, and he makes some excellent points about what it means to belong to this God who gave his only Son as an atonement for our sins and how we treat it so casually.

"The whole transaction of religious conversion has been made mechanical and spiritless.

Faith may now be exercised without a jar to the moral life and without embarrassment to

the Adamic ego. Christ may be received without creating any special love for Him in the

soul of the receiver. The man is 'saved,' but he is not hungry nor thirsty after God."[1]

I think the real show of true grit is to love Jesus with all your heart and not be afraid to live like you do. Yes, you will be challenged, laughed at, even persecuted. But, in the end, you will have raised yourself to a level of commitment, joy, and peace like no other. As Paul says to the Roman church, "O the depth of the riches both of the wisdom and knowledge of God!"

Pursue God; get to know him at a level that continuously challenges everything you already know about him.

Prayer: Lord God, place in my heart the true need to pursue you. Amen.

---

[1]   A. W. Tozer, *The Pursuit of God* (Harrisburg, PA: Christian Publications, Inc.1948), 78.

Being a Bondservant

*If you buy a Hebrew slave, he shall serve for six years; but on the seventh he shall go out as a free man without payment. But if the slave plainly says, 'I love my master, my wife and my children; I will not go out as a free man... then his master shall bring him to God, then he shall bring him to the door or the doorpost. And his master shall pierce his ear with an awl; and he shall serve him permanently.* (Exodus 21: 2, 5-6)

This scripture defines a bondservant; he is someone who could go his own way but loves his master so much he chooses to remain a slave. Note that it's a choice, a conscious choice. Think of Jesus as the master, and we are his bondservants – willingly choosing to remain obedient and a slave to him and his Word.

In Romans 1:1 of the New American Standard (NAS) version, Paul calls himself a bondservant of Jesus. Read Titus 1: 1- 3. Again, the NAS uses the term bondservant. Other versions use the term servant, but no matter which one you read, Paul is an excellent example. He has "sold out" completely for Jesus. After his encounter with Christ on the road to Damascus (Acts 9), Paul never looked back. He claimed his new life in Christ and pledged to be his servant (his bondservant) forever.

Ask yourself, "Whom do I serve?" Now you need to go deeper and ask, "Whose bondservant am I?" Remember the grace Jesus offers is completely free. It is a gift. And it is for everyone! If for no other reason, I should be a bondservant of Christ. He gave everything for me – and you.

Think carefully of what it means to be a bondservant of Christ:

- It is something we are, not something we do.
- It is something we choose.

- We study his Word so we can serve our Master and his creation better.
- We worship him so he knows how wonderful we think he is.
- We will do the most menial task to show our Master how openly and unreservedly we serve him.
- We submit to him as Master of all we are and do.

It's not enough to just surrender our sin to the Lord; we have to surrender our very being. We have to become submissive, obedient, loving bondservants.

Prayer: Lord, I am your bondservant. Place in me your will for my life. Amen.

Heaven or Hell?

*For the message of the cross is foolishness to those who are perishing, but to us who are being saved it is the power of God.* (1Corinthians 1:18)

This passage was the foundation for the message our pastor gave yesterday. Although he went on to expound on Isaiah 29, I am taking a little different route.

This scripture got me to thinking about the people in my life who aren't yet believers. I am saddened by their diminishing, and, in some cases, outright rejection of the truth of salvation.

In this passage Paul is telling the Corinthians that their efforts in sharing the gospel must be based on the message of the cross, not man. Of course others will see Jesus' dying on a cross as foolishness. They lack the Holy Spirit who gives us discernment to see the message of the cross as the ultimate in sacrifice for our own sakes. I too once thought the whole idea of turning my life over to the Lord as foolishness. Who would do that, give your life over to someone you aren't sure even exists? But now I know the truth: Jesus died for me. He answered my call for his care, and my eyes were opened to the power of God.

I'm not sure what non-believers think of me and are just too polite to say. Am I delusional? Am I just naïve? Do I cling to Jesus as a crutch? Or, worst of all to them, am I intellectually challenged? Let me assure you I am not. I am well-read, politically astute (depending upon your own political leanings), can hold my own in most philosophical discussions, and the last time I checked in full possession of all my faculties. So, I am not intellectually challenged or delusional or any of those other things.

I am, however, fascinated by the people who reject the good news because they see themselves as intellectually superior. What a waste of good thinking! We are never too enlightened to ignore the knowledge of our own sin. I challenge you to read how these scholars and statesmen based their beliefs in the one and only Savior: C.S Lewis, Abraham Lincoln, Thomas Jefferson, George Washington, St. Augustine. And then through the eyes of ordinary people who lived their faith under extraordinary circumstances: Corrie Ten Boom, Fanny Crosby, John Wesley, Harriet Beecher Stowe, and others. Just google them; there is information to keep you challenged for months!

You have probably heard the phrase "the distance between heaven and hell is 12 inches." It's the distance between your head and your heart. In this case it is wiser to listen to your heart than your head; give your heart to Jesus and experience the joy he brings with him. Then you can focus on using your head to learn as much as you can about his life and teachings. It will feed your soul as well as quench your thirst for knowledge.

And, yes, I know all about the so-called Christians who behave in abominable ways. True followers of Christ would never sanction violence as a way to build the Kingdom. "They will know we are Christians by our love" is not just a catchy phrase. It is the way we must view our role in a broken world.

Heaven or hell? It's up to you.

Prayer: I choose heaven, Lord. Make me your own. Amen.

How Much is Enough?

*What good will it be for a man if he gains the whole world, yet forfeits his soul? Or what can a man give in exchange for his soul? For the Son of Man is going to come in his Father's glory with his angels, and then he will reward each person according to what he has done.* (Matthew 16:26 – 27)

My friend David is a wise man; he can distill some very complicated ideas into a single thought. And make me think very hard about what it means. He said to me once not too long ago, "Have you reached the point in your life that you don't buy things just to have them?" I answered that I thought I had. Now I'm not so sure. Do I really **need** anything else?

No, I don't; do you?

We live in a culture that tells us to "live out loud." We are bombarded on a minute-to-minute basis with advertising everything you could possibly want. Shopping is a national past time. The more stuff, the better. But, it's nothing new. Read the parable of the rich fool in Luke 12: 13 – 21. He has so much stuff he has to build bigger barns to hold it all.

And, as Jesus points out to him (and us) – "who gets it all when you are dead?" We would be better off to share what we have, serve God the best we can, and focus on others rather than ourselves.

There is an old joke that goes "How much of his money did Rockefeller leave? All of it." Don't get me wrong; I like money and stuff as much as the next person. We have spent the last forty years working and saving to give our children a leg up in the world. I hope though that the Lord means more to me than money and goods. I want to be able to say that I can give it all up for Him if it is required of me.

If your soul should be required of you this very night, where will your "store of goods" be? Are you rich in things or rich in God? Again, the answer you give determines where you will spend eternity. If you are only rich in things and do not know Jesus as your Savior, you won't be receiving your reward from His hand.

Remember, eternity is a very, very, very long time.

And you won't have any of your stuff.

Prayer: Lord, help me to remember who owns me and all I have. Amen.

Life and Death

*And we know that all things work together for good to them that love the Lord and are called according to his purpose.* (Romans 8:28)

When I was eighteen, I was diagnosed with ulcerative colitis. It is an auto-immune disease that attacks the colon. There is no known cause and no cure. It can be controlled in some cases with medications, but sometimes it progresses to the point where surgery is required.

And, for me, that surgery was the only solution. So, on February 14, 1980, I had what is called a complete colectomy; i.e., removal of my entire colon (and part of my small intestine). Think for a minute what that meant, how devastating the news was for me. I was going to have a procedure that made people recoil in disgust. There would be no reversal of this surgery, no hope of going back to "normal."

I was twenty-nine. I had two small children. My son turned five while I was in the hospital, and my daughter was seventeen months. When I left for the hospital, it was all I could do to walk out that door and leave them.

It was a big deal.

I remember lying alone in my hospital bed the night before the surgery and thinking about my husband and how he would cope with everything if I didn't make it. I had been given a 50/50 chance of surviving mostly because of other complications related to the illness. As you can imagine, I could have gone over the edge. Fear gave way to panic, and panic turned to sheer terror at the thought of what lay ahead. But, as he promised, the Lord wrapped his arms around me and brought peace. I can't explain exactly how or when it happened, but I knew he was there in the room with me. I felt his assurance that I would survive, even thrive after it was all said and done.

And, I did. It is one of the reasons that nothing or no one can shake my faith. I have been to the mountain top and have seen his glory. He is real, not some vision or imagined manifestation. He worked in me to bring everything that had happened to good – for me and others with whom I have shared my experience and who have faced the same fears. I am not ashamed or embarrassed about my condition; it is what it is – life saving surgery that I am thankful for every day. There is nothing like facing your own mortality to bring the important things into sharp focus.

When you are facing your last moments, you are likely to only think about three things: whom you loved, who loved you, and what you have done to make a difference. Amen to that! I don't remember worrying about the career I hadn't had yet, the things I didn't have or the places I had never been. I hadn't even had much time to serve the Lord. I just wanted to get well and go home.

Because of the Lord's healing power, I have seen my children grow up, shared in their happiest moments and been blessed with our beautiful grandchildren. It's all frosting on top of the saving grace of Jesus who loved me and gave his life for me.

Prayer: Thank you, Jesus, for your saving grace. Amen.

## Boundaries

*The LORD God took the man and put him in the Garden of Eden to work it and take care of it. And the LORD God commanded the man, "You are free to eat from any tree in the garden; but you must not eat from the tree of the knowledge of good and evil, for when you eat from it you will certainly die." (Gen 3: 15 – 17)*

*And God spoke all these words, saying: "I am the Lord your God, who brought you out of the land of Egypt, out of the house of bondage.*

1. *You shall have no other gods before me.*
2. *You shall not make for yourself any carved image, or any likeness of anything that is in heaven above, or that is in the earth beneath, or that is in the water under the earth; you shall not bow down to them nor serve them. For I, the Lord your God, am a jealous God, visiting the iniquity of the fathers on the children to the third and fourth generations of those who hate me, but showing mercy to thousands, to those who love Me and keep My commandments.*
3. *You shall not take the name of the Lord your God in vain, for the Lord will not hold him guiltless who takes His name in vain.*
4. *Remember the Sabbath day, to keep it holy. Six days you shall labor and do all your work, but the seventh day is the Sabbath of the Lord your God. In it you shall do no work: you, nor your son, nor your daughter, nor your manservant, nor your maidservant, nor your cattle, nor your stranger who is within your gates. For in six days the Lord made the heavens and the earth, the sea, and all that is in them, and rested the seventh day. Therefore the Lord blessed the Sabbath day and hallowed it.*
5. *Honor your father and your mother, that your days may be long upon the land which the Lord your God is giving you.*
6. *You shall not murder.*

7. *You shall not commit adultery.*
8. *You shall not steal.*
9. *You shall not bear false witness against your neighbor.*
10. *You shall not covet your neighbor's house; you shall not covet your neighbor's wife, nor his manservant, nor his maidservant, nor his ox, nor his donkey, nor anything that is your neighbor's.*
(Exodus 20: 1 – 17)

*No, in all these things we are more than conquerors through him who loved us. For I am sure that neither death nor life, nor angels nor rulers, nor things present nor things to come, nor powers, nor height nor depth, nor anything else in all creation, will be able to separate us from the love of God in Christ Jesus our Lord.* (Romans 8:37-39)

Boundaries are important in our lives; they let others know what the limits are as to what we are willing to say, do, think and accept. We talk all the time about setting boundaries – in our lives, our communities, even our countries.

But have you thought about the boundaries God has set for us? He clearly tells Adam and Eve not to eat of the tree of the knowledge of good and evil. But they were convinced that God didn't really mean what he said, and they learned the painful lesson of stepping outside of God's boundaries. Of course in our 20/20 hindsight, we ask why couldn't they see that God had set those limits for their own good?

Read on. In Exodus, God gives Moses direct orders – ten of them – to share with His people so they could live long lives in the land God had chosen for them. Moses didn't even make it down the hill with the stone tablets before the Israelites were building altars to false gods and fashioning golden calves and giving the Egyptians the credit for their release from bondage. We are astounded when we read these words! How dense are these people? He parted the sea for crying out loud. But the people hardened their hearts, and for 400 years, God was silent.

God sets boundaries for our own good. He doesn't leave out any tiny little rule to trip us up. He sees our own misguided attempts to rule our lives and lovingly calls us back to the path he has set for each of us. But, do we listen? NO. We're too busy justifying why we do the things we do, why we sin, why we don't have to believe the Bible, why it isn't our fault that we can't follow the rules. We bumble along the edge of the boundaries, cross back and forth at will and expect God to pick up the pieces and make us whole again.

And he does. In fact, God wanted our joy to be so complete that he sent his own Son to die for us, a Son whose love knows no boundaries for those who call on him. No four hundred years of silence – unless you aren't listening. Contrast the boundaries in Genesis and Exodus with the boundless love expressed in Romans 8. We are so blessed to live in a time when all we have to do is reach out to Jesus, and he is there. We don't have to burn sacrifices on an altar or bring our first fruits from the harvest to try to get right with God. We just have to realize that we are sinners and call on the name of Jesus to save us.

Then you will be heaven-bound, not earth-bound – what a difference!

Prayer: Lord, I accept the boundaries you have defined for me. I want to live within them and show others how wonderful you are. Amen.

The Jubilee

*If you sell or buy property from one of your countrymen, don't cheat him. Calculate the purchase price on the basis of the number of years since the Jubilee. He is obliged to set the sale price on the basis of the number of harvests remaining until the next Jubilee. The more years left, the more money; you can raise the price. But the fewer years left, the less money; decrease the price. What you are buying and selling in fact is the number of crops you're going to harvest. Don't cheat each other. Fear your God. I am God, your God.* (Leviticus 25:14 The Message)

Jubilee was a designated year of rest for the Israelites who reached the Promised Land. They were to plant and harvest for six years, but in the seventh year, they were to rest. It sounds like a good rest for the land as well as the people. We don't seem to understand this concept in today's rush-rush world. There is no rest, just more work. It's one of the things I don't miss about my job.

I remember when I was growing up in the 1950's we still followed the "Blue Laws" which legislated that no business could be conducted on a Sunday. They were designed to help those who wanted to observe Sundays as a day of rest. The only blue law still in effect in Illinois is the one restricting car dealers from conducting business on Sunday. In a way I think it might be good to legislate a day of rest. We might be able to slow down a little and reflect on what the Lord has done for us the previous week.

It would certainly be a departure from the "what-else-can-I-get-done-this-weekend" lifestyle most of us live. However, when God decreed both the Sabbath and the Jubilee, he expected that his people would be grateful for an "ordained" respite from their daily grind. Somehow we have missed the point of his caring and allowed anything to draw us away from a time of rest and reflection, praise and worship, even pausing to acknowledge who has sustained us for the past week.

What if we stopped going out to eat or shopping or going to the movies on Sundays? Would our economy collapse? Probably not. You're saying to yourself right now, "but I like to eat out on Sundays." I'm likely to be at the next table so don't think I've got a handle on this rest thing. It is surely a step-by-step process that requires each of us to make some difficult choices. Just think about it. Maybe you can start with giving more of your Sunday to the Lord and less to the merchants. At some point you might find rest is the very thing you needed all along.

Just food for thought.

Prayer: Lord God, Maker of heaven and earth, create in me a longing for rest on Sundays. Amen.

## Generations

*Not one of these — not one of this evil generation — shall see the good land that I swore to give to your ancestors...* (Deuteronomy 1: 19 – 40)

*For the LORD is good and his love endures forever; his faithfulness continues through all generations.* (Psalm 100:5)

In the book of Deuteronomy, the Lord has grown weary of the lack of obedience in his people. Here they are on the edge of the Promise Land, and they are still whining about what might happen to them if they cross over and anger the Amorites. Moses tells them that the Lord will go before them, that they cannot lose the battle because he is with them. But they don't listen. The Lord's anger extends to each one of the current generation: they will not see the Promised Land. The Israelites cannot enter this beautiful and prosperous land "flowing with milk and honey" because they didn't trust God enough to protect them. And remember, this is the same God who had guided them through the wilderness with a pillar of fire by night and a cloud by day.

Well, duh, you say. How could they be so dense? What will it take for them to see the power of the Lord who will sustain them, protect them, lead them to a better life? What indeed?

The same God who brought them out of Egypt and led them through the wilderness is the same one who held them in that wilderness until the last member of this generation was dead. He means business.

He was so serious about saving this ragtag band of refugees, this slightly more than worthless bunch of misfits that he eventually sent his own Son to save their sorry butts. And they still didn't listen. There were fourteen generations between Abraham and David, fourteen generations between David and the exile to Babylon, and fourteen generations from Babylon to Jesus.

Exactly how many generations will it take to recognize the sovereignty and power of God?

Well, we're still counting. It seems that no amount of miracles, testimonies, near death experiences, or heart-to-heart encounters can convince us once and for all that Christ, Son of the Living God, is alive and caring for us every day. We search out all kinds of excuses, semi-religious organizations, possessions, drugs, televangelists, and our own inner strength in a vain attempt to fill that nagging void in our hearts.

And the answer to our pain is the same as it was for the generation of wilderness wanderers: a faithful God whose love endures forever.

Prayer: Lord, please stop my wandering. I want to be yours, now and forever. Amen.

Make Every Minute Count

Read Luke 23

Luke 23 is Luke's account of the trial and crucifixion of Jesus. As I was reading this chapter, there were things that struck me that I hadn't really noticed before. Most importantly, I saw how Jesus made every minute count, even when he was on the cross. Here are some of the things he did in the very last minutes of his life:

- Fulfilled the Scripture's prophecy of his death.
- Provided for his mother's care.
- Reassured his followers.
- Secured the future of the thief on the cross next to him.
- Set an example for surrendering all to the Father.
- Took on the sins of the world.
- Removed the barrier of blood sacrifice for sins.

Makes me feel a little inadequate. Of course we haven't been called to save the souls of eternity, but we can do so much with what we have – especially the time we have. We can make every minute count for Christ:

- Acknowledge his presence in your life.
- Treat others as you know he would want you to.
- Remember the sacrifice he made for you.
- Make his love the filter for <u>all</u> of your interactions.
- Look for ways to serve him – even the smallest gesture can make a big difference to someone who is in need.
- Love him; worship him; praise him.

We can easily focus on the resurrection. But Jesus did so much more for us. "God made him who had no sin to be sin for us, so that in him we might become the righteousness of God." (2 Corinthians 5:21)

We owe him everything; we paid nothing.

Prayer: Christ is dead. Christ has risen. Christ will come again. Amen.

## Q & A

*Do not let your hearts be troubled. You believe in God; believe also in me.*

*My Father's house has many rooms; if that were not so, would I have told you that I am going there to prepare a place for you? And if I go and prepare a place for you, I will come back and take you to be with me that you also may be where I am. You know the way to the place where I am going. Thomas said to him, "Lord, we don't know where you are going, so how can we know the way?" Jesus answered, "I am the way and the truth and the life. No one comes to the Father except through me. If you really know me, you will know my Father as well. From now on, you do know him and have seen him." (John 14: 1 – 7)*

The Thursday before Easter is known as Maundy Thursday. It is from the Latin phrase: novum mandatum which means new covenant. When Jesus broke the bread and drank from the cup at what we know as The Last Supper, he told the disciples that his spilled blood would create a new covenant.

Christ's sacrifice would now be the means to redemption. No more lambs, doves or burnt offerings to get right with God. And then he tells them he must go away for a while, but he will return for them.

The timing of this conversation is important to note since it is one of the key teaching moments Jesus shares with his disciples. They have just finished the last supper he will share with them before his crucifixion; he knows hard times are ahead, and he wants to reassure them that he won't forsake them. No matter what happens over the next few days, Jesus wants them to know he won't forget them and neither will his Father.

And, because they were his followers, they would know the way to go. The disciples weren't ready to hear about the Cross, betrayal, or a big change in the way they would live their faith. They were still trying to process the fact that Jesus had washed their feet like a common servant. Now he was telling them not to worry when he left them. Panic was beginning to set in along with those uneasy feelings of confusion and dread.

So Thomas puts words to the thoughts they are all having: "Lord, we <u>don't</u> know where you are going, so how can we know the way?" (Underline, mine) And Jesus answers with the words many of us know so well: "I am the way, the truth and the life." If you read verse five truly as a question, verse six becomes the answer. Emphasize the "I" and you will see what I mean.

I wonder if Jesus is just a little exasperated at this point – like, "c'mon, guys, don't you get it? I've been telling you for the last three years that I am in the Father, and the Father is in me. Can we make a leap here to the obvious conclusion?" With everything else Jesus has to be concerned with at this point, he doesn't need thick-headed disciples who can't keep up.

Don't you think God might be just a little impatient with us as well? He has provided every answer to every question we have through his Son. But we keep trying to discount Jesus, argue scripture, make excuses for our lack of faith and generally ignore the basic truth: Jesus gave his life on the Cross to save you and me.

It should be obvious.

Prayer: Jesus, please give me a renewed heart for you. Increase my faith, Lord. Amen.

## In the Beginning

*In the beginning was the Word, and the Word was with God, and the Word was God. [2] He was with God in the beginning. [3] Through him all things were made; without him nothing was made that has been made.* (John 1: 1- 3)

I was driving home one day and heard a statement on the radio that caught my attention: He began the beginning in the beginning before the beginning began to be. Say that fast three times! It was right before Easter, and it got me to thinking about all Jesus represents. He was with God in the beginning; he was there at the earth's formation and its subsequent evolving into what he had planned all along. He came to earth as a human to suffer for our sins. He witnessed your birth and mine. He has loved us all as only he can do.

And what have we done for him? Mocked his Word, used his name in vain, ignored his teachings, slandered his chosen people. But to be fair, many of us have surrendered our lives to him, worked in his name, and given generously to his cause. Unfortunately, we have done many of these things for our own glory and purposes. Read Psalm 139, especially verses 23 and 24. Ask the Lord to search your heart and uncover any false motives, selfish desires, or offensive ways. You'll be surprised (or maybe not) at what the Lord brings to mind.

We can count on these basic truths to convict us of our selfish thoughts and motives:

- God is not mocked.
- You can't out-give God.
- Jesus is the way, the truth and the life.
- Be sure that your sin will find you out.
- God knows your thoughts before you do.

The bottom line is that if you think you are fooling anyone, least of all God, you need to re-examine your life. He knows everything about you from the beginning; he loves you; he will never leave you.

Hold onto those basic truths as well and know they will guide you away from sin and into the light – a luminous glow that shines brighter than any earthly light: "In him was life, and that life was the light of all mankind. The light shines in the darkness, and the darkness has not overcome it." (John 1: 4 – 5)

And it never will.

Prayer: Lord, let your light shine in my heart. Cleanse me and make me your own. Amen.

## Spring Pruning

*I am the true vine, and my Father is the gardener. He cuts off every branch in me that bears no fruit, while every branch that does bear fruit he prunes so that it will be even more fruitful. You are already clean because of the word I have spoken to you. Remain in me, as I also remain in you. No branch can bear fruit by itself; it must remain in the vine. Neither can you bear fruit unless you remain in me.* (John 15: 1 – 4)

Our knockout roses are about to burst into bloom, the earliest I have ever seen. My husband prunes them in early spring just as the new growth is starting to appear. And his pruning really pays off in the number of new buds we see. On the side of the garage at our first house was a climbing rose. We moved in the end of March, and that rose bush looked pretty sick that year, overgrown with dead branches and very few blooms. So we decided to cut it to the ground and see if it really needed to be removed. While drastic, it was just what that rose bush needed. You have never seen a fuller, more beautiful, brilliantly red rose bush. From a little stub to a magnificent bush that grew taller than the trellis to which it was attached.

In this passage, Jesus is using visuals that the disciples' Jewish heritage can support. Israel had long been known as God's vineyard. In the Old Testament, many of the prophets referred to Israel as God's vine, but it is also recorded that they let that vine become overgrown, mixed with other bloodlines and run wild.

The Jews of Jesus' time thought being Jewish was all they needed to be in God's family. But Jesus drops the big bomb that HE is the true vine, and unless they remain faithful to him, they are not part of God's family. They not only needed to believe in the true vine, they needed to accept that God was going to prune those useless branches that could not or would not bear fruit for Jesus. (Think Pharisees and the Sanhedrin, governing body of the Jews at that time.)

And just like that rose bush, God prunes us. At the center of it all is Jesus – the vine, the one true vine. Every saved heart is part of that vine. Fruit cannot spring up on its own; it cannot be disconnected from the main vine and live and bear more fruit.

And so it is with us. We cannot bring others to Christ if we aren't connected directly to him through our own salvation. Our lives become examples of living in the grace of a just and loving God who takes care of his own, even to the point of cutting us down to a stub so we can grow back into what he intended.

But when we remain in Christ – confess him as Savior, follow him, love him, witness for him, serve him – he allows us to branch out and bring others to know his love and grace.

Prayer: Lord, I am ready to branch out and share my love for you. Amen.

Who's on First?

*Seek ye first the kingdom of God, and all these things will be added unto you.* (Matthew 6:33)

*For where your treasure is, there your heart will be also.* (Matthew 6:21)

*Let us not become weary in doing good, for at the proper time we will reap a harvest if we do not give up.* (Galatians 6:9)

Here is some helpful advice for all of you: Put God first. I've said it before, and I'll keep saying it until we all are able to truly believe this commitment is the only way to live the abundant life Jesus promised us. He didn't promise a problem-free life. He promised us an abundant life – in Him. Apart from his love and care, we cannot process all that comes at us in a lifetime of work, family, relationships and problems.

When I tell you to put God first, I'm not talking about what you buy or give away; what you think you need to do to be happy. I'm talking about the minute-to-minute life you live. I'm talking about the determination and faith it takes to live every one of those minutes for Christ.

Think about your worst fear. What can you do to manage that fear? It's not about ignoring it, pushing it down to the depths of your insides, or worrying about it hoping to stave off the possibility. Imagining the worst scenario will never prepare you for a reality that may come. The fear is what haunts you and keeps you from finding peace.

Now, put your worst fear in the context of God's love for you. Think carefully and prayerfully about what those words mean. Who is your strength? Can any human fill the role of keeping you going when you have to face your worst fear? In most cases, those who would be your strength may be hurting as much as you are. No, the only one who can rescue you is Jesus Christ. The One who gave his very life for you and me is the One who can bring you back from the brink of despair.

If you have learned to put God first, you have the most powerful ally there ever was/is. You will suffer, no doubt, but you must call out to Jesus. He will do as he promised and not forsake you. Remember to whom you surrender all – your fears, your dreams, your sins, your life.

Everything. Every day. Every minute.

Prayer: Lord, help me to live for you every minute. Amen.

## Standard Issue

*Therefore I love thy commandments above gold; yea, above fine gold.*
(Psalm 119:127)

I remember my dad talking about his army days and the items he received, compliments of the US government. He called them "standard issue." Everyone got the same things, regardless of how or when they became a part of the infantry. But, one thing was for certain: every item had a function. Each one was put in his hands to assist him in making it through basic training, transport to a foreign land and ultimately into battle.

The Lord's standard issue is the 10 Commandments. It doesn't matter when you read, study or learn them by heart. Each one has a function and is written to assist us in living a life that honors God.

1. *You shall have no other gods before me.*
2. *You shall not make for yourself any carved image, or any likeness of anything that is in heaven above, or that is in the earth beneath, or that is in the water under the earth; you shall not bow down to them nor serve them. For I, the Lord your God, am a jealous God, visiting the iniquity of the fathers on the children to the third and fourth generations of those who hate me, but showing mercy to thousands, to those who love Me and keep My commandments.*
3. *You shall not take the name of the Lord your God in vain, for the Lord will not hold him guiltless who takes His name in vain.*
4. *Remember the Sabbath day, to keep it holy. Six days you shall labor and do all your work, but the seventh day is the Sabbath of the Lord your God. In it you shall do no work: you, nor your son, nor your daughter, nor your manservant, nor your maidservant, nor your cattle, nor your stranger who is within your gates. For*

*in six days the Lord made the heavens and the earth, the sea, and all that is in them, and rested the seventh day. Therefore the Lord blessed the Sabbath day and hallowed it.*

5.   *Honor your father and your mother, that your days may be long upon the land which the Lord your God is giving you.*

6.   *You shall not murder.*

7.   *You shall not commit adultery.*

8.   *You shall not steal.*

9.   *You shall not bear false witness against your neighbor.*

10.  *You shall not covet your neighbor's house; you shall not covet your neighbor's wife, nor his manservant, nor his maidservant, nor his ox, nor his donkey, nor any thing that is your neighbor's.*

Paul reminds us in his letter to the Romans that although we are saved from the punishment of the law, those very commandments reveal to us what sin is. Read them again. Is there a life topic that isn't covered in those ten verses? Is there any reason you wouldn't want to live in obedience to every one? No. We can rejoice in the fact that we are saved, and we can rejoice in the fact that God has given us these clear instructions.

Each commandment is a standard by which we can live our lives in obedience to God. We do have the advantage of having Jesus as our Advocate when we break a commandment, but you have to admit, just following this blueprint would ensure a pretty good life. And, while we're on that subject, wouldn't it be wonderful if everyone followed these commandments? Unfortunately, in our human condition, we don't have the capacity to achieve that level of righteousness.

But, we can try.

Prayer: Dear Jesus, thank you for providing this blueprint for my life. Help me to follow it every day. Amen.

No Badge of Honor

*Put on the full armor of God, so that you can take your stand against the devil's schemes.* (Ephesians 6:11)

*Naked into this world you came, and naked you will depart.* (Job 1:21)

I know so many people who wear their doubts about the existence of God like a badge of honor. They want so much to set themselves apart, feel special and show their differences proudly. Well guess what? It's no badge of honor to live without the Lord. In fact, it leaves you vulnerable as the day you were born.

Naked.

Nothing to protect you from the elements or from the assault Satan is planning for you on a daily basis.

You need God's protection; you need Jesus to stand against the devil's schemes. What is the full armor of God? Read on.

"Stand firm then, with the belt of truth buckled around your waist, with the breastplate of righteousness in place, and with your feet fitted with the readiness that comes from the gospel of peace. In addition to all this, take up the shield of faith, with which you can extinguish all the flaming arrows of the evil one. Take the helmet of salvation and the sword of the Spirit, which is the word of God." (Ephesians 6: 15 – 17)

Protection doesn't mean the arrows of lies, the sword of deceit, or the hammer of pain won't attack you. The difference is that your armor will be in place to withstand the assaults. You may be battered and bruised for a time, but the Holy Spirit will be right by your side to comfort you and build you back up.

Nothing can prevail against the power of God. Nothing. Not even death. The only time you will be free from the slings and arrows is in heaven, when you are eternally safe in the arms of Jesus.

So, naked you come into the world, dressed in the armor of God, you live in the world, and naked you return to the safety of heaven where your armor is no longer needed.

Prayer: Jesus, please be my badge of honor. Amen.

Be a Man.

*When I was a child, I talked like a child, I thought like a child, I reasoned like a child. When I became a man, I put the ways of childhood behind me.* (1Corinthians 13:11)

Our grandson, Aidan (7), explaining growing up to his brother, Jonas(6): "Be a man, Jonas. Sit up, eat your vegetables, try new things. That's how you be a man." And that's just one of the many pearls of wisdom Aidan offers on a regular basis. You have to admit it's good advice.

I would add a couple of things. Repent and believe. Remember Romans 10:9 & 10: "If you confess with your lips and believe in your heart that Jesus was raised from the dead, you will be saved." Confess means repent; believe in your heart means sincerely giving your very life source to Jesus.

It seems like a paradox when you think how Jesus talked about becoming like children in order to enter his kingdom. How can you reduce yourself to a childlike state and still put away childish things? I think it's a matter of sequence. Because, out of that paradox comes the enduring truth that at some point you have to be a man; you have to grow up in your faith. You may start out with the innocence of a child, but eventually, you will reach a point where you need to make decisions, witness, and live your faith like a man/woman. You leave that childish state and move on to growing in your knowledge of and commitment to Christ.

Continuing on to verse twelve, Paul reminds the Corinthians that now they see dimly what will be made clear to them when they (all of us) are made perfect in the day of Jesus Christ. We can only understand so much, but what we do understand is the importance of living for Jesus and yearning for the day when he returns.

Be ready.

Be a man.

Prayer: I want to be ready, Lord. Help me renew my commitment to you. Amen.

Separate but Equal

*Two other men, both criminals, were also led out with him to be executed. When they came to the place called the Skull, they crucified him there, along with the criminals—one on his right, the other on his left.* (Luke 23: 32 – 33)

We attended our friends' church last week, and as I sat listening to the sermon, I looked over to the far wall and saw three wooden crosses hanging there. At first, I thought the middle cross was higher than the other two, but it was actually at the same height. Of course I had seen them there before, but this time I began to think about the significance of their being at the same height.

When Jesus was crucified, he was hung in the middle between two thieves. At that point no one saw him as the Savior of the world. They considered him no better or no worse, just equal to any criminal. He would die a common death with common men on a common cross. His only moment of separating himself from the others was when Jesus promised one of the thieves (the one who defended his innocence) that indeed he would be with Jesus in paradise that very day.

Think about that phrase "with Jesus in paradise." Who would believe that? It is ridiculous really. Here they were at the most dire moments of their lives, and Jesus promises paradise. All that thief had to say was "remember me when you come into your kingdom," and he was given that promise from the very lips of Jesus Christ.

Let's break it down a little more. First, the thief had to believe that Jesus was who he said he was. Second, he had to believe there would actually be a kingdom. Third, he had to believe Jesus would rule in that kingdom ("when you come into <u>your</u> kingdom"). Add to that the fact Jesus had not even been raised from the dead, and yet this common thief believed there was a better place wherever Jesus would be.

There is a better place. It is just a matter of accepting who is there waiting for us. Jesus promised forgiveness, acceptance, eternal life. We are all equal in our sin and need for his forgiveness. All we have to do is exactly what that thief did.

Believe.

Simple, ridiculously simple.

Prayer: Lord, help my unbelief. Amen.

Power to the People

*For to be sure, he (Christ) was crucified in weakness, yet he lives by God's power. Likewise, we are weak in him, yet by God's power we will live with him to serve you. Examine yourselves to see whether you are living in the faith. Test yourselves.* (2Corinthians 13:4 – 5)

Are you living in the faith? Take this test:

1. What are your core beliefs?
2. Is Christ your top priority?
3. Is serving Christ your goal?
4. Are you living a life that commends you to God?
5. Is Christ living in you?

Realizing that Christ died for you and giving him the power in your life proves that you are saved, but does it prove Christ is living in you? What evidence can you present that shows you are living in the faith?

Tough questions.

Paul's entreaty to the church in Corinth is that they will continue in their faith and not fail the test of living for Christ. In fact, he tells them they are to draw on the power of God through Jesus Christ to keep from doing wrong.

Do you ever think about the power you have, power given to you by God himself? How can that be? I think I'm pretty ordinary; I'm just one of the multitudes. But the truth is that I have the power of God. He is on my side. What shall I do with this power? The answer is whatever God tells me to do with it.

Just like the Corinthians, I get off track. I forget whom I serve. I forget I am an example to others of what being a Christian really is. But God always calls me back, reminds me what I have to do, and touches my heart in a way that leaves no doubt how much he loves me. I cannot ignore his call.

I am the first to admit I minimize the power of God, mostly because I want to fit him into what I can understand. Fortunately, he doesn't care what I think about his power. He is who he is, and I am very grateful for that. He works in me for HIS good purpose, not the other way around. I want to live in the faith; I want to make living in the faith my top priority; I want to acknowledge the power of God in my life.

And I'm going to keep telling myself that until I am unable to say it or think it.

Prayer: Father God, remind of the power I have through You. Amen.

Desperately Seeking Jesus

*For the Son of Man came to seek and to save what was lost.* (Luke 19:10)

*And without faith it is impossible to please God, because anyone who comes to him must believe that he exists and that he rewards those who earnestly seek him.* (Hebrews 11:6)

The verses above emphasize the need to see the whole of an idea and not just one side or the other. There is an ongoing discussion among Christians as to whether Jesus is seeking us, or we are seeking him. I think it is both.

Look at Luke 19:10. "For the Son of Man came to seek and to save the lost."

This gospel passage clearly states that Jesus is seeking us. He came to seek and to save. He knows our every need, and he knows us to the very depth of our souls. He is constantly calling to us, showing us the way to eternal life with him.

Now read again Hebrews 11: 6. This verse represents the other side of the coin. NOW that you have been found and responded to Jesus' call to you as a sinner, you must acknowledge his power in your life and seek his guidance for living a life that pleases him.

There is a danger in seeking Jesus before we know him as Savior. Many times as we search for answers to life's most difficult circumstances, we fall into the trap of looking for the easy way out. Thinking that Jesus is available to fix our problems and rescue us from unhappiness sets us up for a shallow, one-sided relationship. We are the engineers, and Jesus is just a tool we use to ease our pain. And, as soon as the storm has passed, we continue to seek other means, other answers to our problems.

However, when we truly believe that Jesus is seeking us (remember, we exist for him, not the other way around), we then know that he is establishing the terms of the relationship. We either accept or reject these terms. We agree to "be found", or we go on searching for our own answers. I think it is the reason so many people fall into a pattern of "seeking". I have had friends over the years who sought peace in Hinduism, strength in Buddhism, acceptance in a cult. They moved from one disappointing lifestyle to another, hoping for a peace that is only available from the Savior of the world.

"Behold, I stand at the door and knock. If any man hears my voice and answers me, I will come in and eat with him and he with me." (Rev 3:20)

"Ask and it will be given to you; seek and ye shall find; knock and the door will be opened to you." (Luke 11: 9)

Two sides of the same coin -- Jesus.

Prayer: Dear Jesus, help me to seek you earnestly in all things. Amen.

Keep on Keepin' On

*Let us not become weary in doing good, for at the proper time we will reap a harvest if we do not give up.* (Galatians 6:9)

From my desk in our sunroom, I can see across many cornfields almost to the next town a few miles away. I love being able to watch as the farmers plant the seeds, as the sprouts show themselves in early spring, and then when the harvest begins. It is so like our own lives -- that cycle of being born, growing, and then our final harvest. It is also very much like the cycle we go through in our Christian lives. The seed is planted in our hearts; we accept Jesus as Savior; we grow in our faith; and finally, we reap the harvest of His love and righteousness. And, if we are true to our beliefs and share the Good News with others, we will someday see the fruits of our labor.

I know sometimes we get tired of trying to live the life of a Believer. It is hard work, and we don't often see the results in the lives of those we witness to -- whether openly or by living in a way that proves a love for the Lord. It can be exhausting. But as Paul tells the Galatians, we can't give up. We must keep on keepin' on. The seed needs to be planted in the hearts of others just as it was planted in ours.

Who first told you about the love of Jesus? About his sacrifice for you? What would have happened to you if that person hadn't bothered?

How have you grown in your faith? Not by yourself, I'm sure. There have been hardworking people who have given time to your Bible study, Sunday school class, sermons, and prayer groups. What would happen if they grew weary in sharing their experiences and love for the Lord? But, thankfully, they don't.

We can do no less.

So, keep up the work of the Lord -- share your story, live as an example so that others will want what you have. And, don't give up! For at the proper time, we will reap a harvest!

Prayer: Lord, keep me going when I want to give up! Amen.

There is Nothing Left to Learn the Hard Way.

*For everything that was written in the past was written to teach us, so that through endurance and the encouragement of the Scriptures we might have hope.* (Romans 15:4)

A friend sent me an email recently that talked about getting old and having nothing left to learn the hard way. I can certainly relate. While I think I still have some time left to enjoy life, I also know that I don't have as long as I did twenty years ago – you know, when I was 40-something and could still learn some hard lessons. As never before, time is of the essence. The Lord says our days are numbered, and only he knows that number.

Romans 15:4 is a wonderful reminder that much of the time I have left needs to be spent relying on the Word of God, not that I don't already try to do that. But I suspect the next twenty years will present their own set of challenges that will require endurance, and most especially, the need for encouragement. And where better to find that encouragement than in God's own sustaining Word?

*For everything that was written in the past was written to teach us…* What have I learned?

- God sent his only Son to die so that I might have eternal life.
- No greater love has a man than to lay down his life for his friends.
- Jesus is the answer to any question I might have.
- Salvation through Christ is my only hope for today and eternity.
- Where does my help come from? My help comes from the Lord who made heaven and earth.
- He who is in me is greater than he who is in the world.
- I can do all things through Christ who strengthens me.

- All things work together for good to them that love the Lord and are called according to His purpose.
- Nothing can separate me from the love of God through Jesus Christ.
- Love one another

…to name a few.

I have learned some of these truths the hard way. I have relied on my own ambition and skills too many times. I have steered the course of my life in the direction I wanted to go, not once asking God if he had the same journey in mind for me.

I have tried to answer the hard questions with worldly wisdom instead of God's Word. I have tried to control my little piece of the world, using my own strength to do the right thing, say the right thing, and believe the right thing – which in many cases was totally the wrong thing.

There is only one way to find and stay the course God has for you and me. Read and study His Word. Read a passage of scripture then listen for God's whisper in your mind. He is there, ready and waiting for each of us to stop long enough to seek His counsel and really listen for it. Be obedient to his leading.

Make your own list of truths. I just wrote from memory; I didn't look up these scriptures. I just let my mind draw out what has meant the most to me. You can do the same. Think about the things you have learned the hard way. How can God speak to you through His Word and encourage you on the way?

Listen.

Prayer: Lord, I am listening for your voice – through others, through your Word and through my prayers. Amen.

Forgiving Hearts

*Bear with each other and forgive whatever grievances you may have against one another. Forgive as the Lord forgave you.* (Colossians 3:13)

When I became a Christian, I asked the Lord to give me a heart of forgiveness. I wanted to be someone who was able to forgive anyone who had hurt me. I admit it was a daunting request. I know the Lord answered my prayer, but I haven't always listened to that heart of forgiveness. I have nursed my hurts and painful memories just like you have. I would find myself crying out to God that I deserved to hold onto my anger, my frustration with so-and-so because… what? That I deserved this indulgence, I had earned it, I hadn't meant what I said in asking for a heart for forgiveness?

None of the above.

When I asked and received the deep conviction to be a forgiving person, I relinquished my right to hold onto those transgressions. No harboring hurts, no building up justification for my anger, no carrying this fake cross. God wants better for me – and for you. I want to be obedient to God's Word. "Forgive one another as I have forgiven you. Short verse; huge message.

If you want God to forgive you, you have to forgive others. It is the truth of His Word. There is no getting around it. And it doesn't matter if others think they need forgiveness or not. YOUR heart must be clean before the Lord if you want him to hear your cries for anything. He doesn't try to make a deal with you; he doesn't try to bring the other person to justice for your convenience. He calls to each of our hearts to confess that we have held a grudge, wanted revenge, or were holding out for an apology.

Forget it; ain't gonna happen.

God is just – that's all we need to know. And if you want him to be just with everyone else, you must accept his justice for yourself. Don't worry about what the other person is going to get; for all you know he has already sought forgiveness in his own prayers. It is not your concern. Your concern is getting right with God through the wonderful forgiveness offered to us through the sacrifice of Jesus on that Cross at Calvary.

Think carefully. Ask God to reveal to you what you might be harboring in your heart against someone else. Let it go. Ask God to give you that forgiving heart even when you don't feel like it.

Determine to be the forgiving person you know you can be.

Determine to enjoy the freedom of losing those hurts and pain.

Prayer: Lord, help me to forgive as you forgive. Amen.

Loving God

*For the man who loves God is known by God.* (1Corinthians 8:3)

I heard a phrase on the radio the other day that struck me with its truth: Love God for who he is, not what he gives. There are so many times we look to God to give us what we want and <u>think</u> we need. And he is so generous with his gifts. He may not always give us the exact thing we ask for, but he always gives us what is best for us.

And so it goes. We ask; he gives generously. We call to him; he answers. We demand his attention; he is always there. No wonder we focus on what he gives. But what if we would focus on who he is MORE than what he gives? Think about the attributes we ascribe to him: omniscient, divine, worthy, loving, etc. These are the words that describe the God we know, usually from personal experience. How many of those attributes do we assign to his giving us what we want? Not very many, and yet we spend an inordinate amount of our prayer time asking for things.

Where is our love for him? Where is our gratitude for his generous spirit? Where is the acknowledgement of his miracles for all mankind? Let's focus on the big picture for just a moment. "For God so loved the world that he gave his only begotten son that whoever believes in him shall not perish but have eternal life." (John 3:16) And that is all we need to say about his giving. Isn't that enough?

The bigger issue is do you believe in a God who is loving, just, holy, all powerful, and peaceful? You have to see all of God to truly understand his generous gifts, most especially the gift of his Son for our salvation. He <u>knows</u> us by our love for him and for each other. And, just as we get to know each other and love each other for who we are, we can get to know God and love him for who he is. What a challenge! Just think how our time with him would change if we saw him as our friend and confidante, not just a father who gives us good things.

So, the next time you are deep into your list of wants, stop and focus on who God is, not just on what he can give.

Prayer: Lord, I do love you for who you are. Help me to focus on that truth. Amen.

Be Mine

*Blessed are those who hear the word of God and obey it.* (Luke 11:28)

The table decorations at the church service we attended yesterday included a bowl of candy conversation hearts. You know the ones; they say love you, sweet, etc. The music director asked us what phrase God would use if he gave us a candy heart. The response was Be Mine. He is always calling to us; he wants us to belong to him.

I thought of some other conversation hearts God could give us:

- Obey
- Love You
- Forgiven
- Blessed
- Serve me
- Trust me
- Prayer
- Follow me

I'm sure you could come up with your own list. We all long for love whether we want to admit it or not. There is a lonely spot in our hearts that only God can fill. He made us that way – with a God-shaped hole in our hearts so that we could ask him to fill it in and then experience the joy of knowing him. There is nothing like it. I remember when I first felt the love of Jesus. It was the warmest, most comforting, most satisfying feeling ever. I knew in that moment I now had the ultimate in love and care.

Forget all those places you have already looked for that kind of love; you will only find it in the salvation Christ offers. Even though we celebrate love on Valentine's Day, romantic love can never fulfill our needs for the love of God through Jesus. Celebrate his love; make it your own. As it says in Luke 11, we can choose to listen to His Word and obey it -- and be blessed.

Reach deep into the bowl of candy hearts and fill your hands with the love of Jesus.

Prayer: Lord, I celebrate your love! Amen.

The Urge to Merge

*Husbands, love your wives, as Christ loved the church and gave himself up for her, that he might sanctify her, having cleansed her by the washing of water with the word, so that he might present the church to himself in splendor, without spot or wrinkle or any such thing, that she might be holy and without blemish. In the same way husbands should love their wives as their own bodies. He who loves his wife loves himself. For no one ever hated his own flesh, but nourishes and cherishes it, just as Christ does the church,* (Ephesians 5: 25 – 33)

June is historically the month for weddings. The June bride was epitomized in movies, magazines and the hearts of young girls when I was growing up. I'm pretty sure no one I knew thought about whether or not her new husband was going to love her as Christ loves his church. It's usually more of "Let's party" and less of "Let's be sure we live up to what Jesus expects".

But the fact remains that if we follow his commands, God will support us in our marriages, friendships, goals, and work. When Paul tells the Ephesian husbands to love their wives as Jesus loves the church and as they love themselves, he is reminding them that there is a standard set for them. This marriage thing isn't just for fun; it's serious business. It is the foundation of the family and future generations who will know and love God as you, husband and wife, have done.

I read an interesting item the other day: It's not about finding the right person; it's about becoming the right person. How can you do that? Find the answers in his Word. It's the manual for life. From beginning to end, The Bible is our guide to abundant living. It is our counsel when we don't know what to do. It is our comfort when times are tough. It is our gateway to knowing Jesus as he wanted us to know him.

So, if someone you know is getting married, you might add a few words of encouragement and our Bible verse to your card of congratulations. They may not take it seriously at the moment, but it will come back to them later, and it might help.

Prayer: Lord, I am thankful that you are making the right person in my marriage so that we don't miss the abundant life you offer. Amen

What does the Lord require of you?

*He has showed you, O man, what is good. And what does the Lord require of you? To act justly and to love mercy and to walk humbly with your God.* (Micah 6: 8)

Several years ago, I had a friend who thought this verse was the one to live by. She argued that it is really enough to act justly, love mercy and walk humbly with God. She thought that seeking salvation was a selfish act which really didn't do anyone any good. In her frustration to make me see her point, she shouted, "All you talk about is save yourself, save yourself. What good does that do? It's so selfish."

I don't think I ever convinced her that salvation was the <u>beginning</u> of my being able to act justly, love mercy and walk humbly. Without the love of Jesus in my heart, I wouldn't be able to sustain the acts of mercy and humility. That love is what takes me out of myself and allows me to give others the love and attention they need. It is truly a selfless act – surrendering everything, holding back nothing.

And, while I fully respect the Old Testament and its teachings, it is still the story of promises unfulfilled. In reality, the best we could do before Jesus was Micah 6:8. We had no other way to show our faithfulness to the Lord. Now we have a Savior who gave his life so that we could live as he taught us to live: Love thy neighbor as thyself.

Without His love in our hearts, we are struggling to act justly, mercifully, and humbly under our own power, let alone give unconditional love to those around us. Impossible! But we are children of the God of the Possible, and He gives us the strength we need just when we need it to persevere in doing good to others.

Let's face it; we're not exactly models of mercy and humility. We fight with each other, put each other down, brag about our accomplishments and generally live for ourselves. The world and its treasures lure us into believing we can have everything, do everything and give back nothing. I'm in it to win it as the saying goes. Love my neighbor? I don't even love myself.

The good news is there is someone who loves you so much that you just might begin to love yourself when you realize what he has done for you. And each step you take in your Christian walk will be better (not necessarily easier) because you know him. Jesus holds your heart and your hand and leads you to loving others, offering them mercy – all with a humble assurance that you can do all things through Christ.

Justice, mercy, and humility; God requires them, and Jesus puts them within our grasp.

Prayer: Lord, I know what you require of me, and I will do my best to be your servant. Amen.

Love one another.

*Dear friends, since God so loved us, we also ought to love one another.*
(1John 4:11)

Jesus calls us to love one another. Sounds easy enough – three little words. He isn't talking about romantic love or how we love our children; he's talking about agape (uh-gop-a) love: open, non-judgmental, warts-and-all kind of love. The essence of agape love is self-sacrifice.

When was the last time you set aside your own needs to show love to someone else - undeserving, radical, selfless love? How many opportunities have you missed?

I was in the drugstore one afternoon when a woman came in asking to rent a wheelchair for her son. She wanted to know if they rented by the week and how much it would cost. The salesman said they weren't renting wheelchairs any longer because the store was closing. But she could buy one, and he told her the price of several models. She shrugged, said thank you and started for the door.

I finished paying for my supplies and went out to the parking lot. The woman was parked next to me and was obviously explaining to her son why she didn't have a wheelchair for him.

I wanted to buy that wheelchair; I could afford it. But fear of being rejected stopped me. What if she didn't want my charity? What if she misunderstood my gesture?

Well, that is something I'll never know. I got into my car and drove away. And have regretted it ever since. I let an obvious opportunity to serve the Lord slip by me. And I beat myself up about it for days.

A couple of months later one of my co-workers lost her home in a house fire. Her husband was just beginning his recovery from cancer treatments, and they were in dire need. I couldn't get down to her boss's office fast enough. I had been carrying around the cash equal to the cost of that wheelchair, and I wasn't going to miss my chance.

Call it guilt; call it penance, call it whatever you want. But recognize there are opportunities every day to serve the Lord by sharing what you have with brothers, sisters, friends or strangers. I am careful these days to be open to His call. No more dithering over details. God will take care of those without my help.

No fear
No judgment
No expectations

Just love.

Prayer: Lord, help me to love others and give generously without worrying about the details. Amen.

Forgiveness as an Act of Love

*If we confess our sins, he is faithful and just to forgive us our sins and cleanse us from all unrighteousness.* (I John 1:9)

When I first became a Christian, one of our neighbors invited me to a Bible Study at her home. This verse was one of the first I memorized. It was amazing to me that God would forgive anything let alone the things **I** had done. I'm sure none of you would think I was all that bad a person, but I knew I wasn't living up to the standards I had set for myself and certainly not the ones my parents had set.

Some form of the word "forgive" appears sixty-three times in the New Testament. We are clear on how Jesus is able to forgive us. Read again our opening verse.

But how do we forgive others?

Matthew 6:12 says, "Forgive us our sins as we forgive those who have sinned against us."

Matthew 6: 14&15 says, "For if you forgive men when they sin against you, your heavenly Father will also forgive you. But if you do not forgive men their sins, your Father will not forgive your sins."

Luke 6: 37a says, "Do not judge, and you will not be judged. Do not condemn, and you will not be condemned. Forgive, and you will be forgiven."

Colossians 3:13 says, "Bear with each other and forgive whatever grievances you may have against one another. Forgive as the Lord forgave you."

Jesus lays out the rule of reciprocity; i.e., this for that. We must forgive in order to be forgiven. Jesus also says we must repent of our sins so that we may be forgiven. So, what do you do with that person who doesn't repent? How can you forgive someone who doesn't acknowledge his own sin against you?

If you really think about it, when you forgive someone, even if they don't ask for it, you are allowing God to work in <u>your</u> heart. He will only be able to work in the hearts of those you forgive if they ask; i.e., it's not your problem. You can release the anger and hurt through your conscious decision to forgive.

Bible teacher Lewis Smedes[2] offers 5 common mistakes people make about the process of forgiving:

1.  Forgiving somebody is excusing them.
2.  Forgiving is the same as tolerance.
3.  People expect instant results.
4.  You have to run to the person and tell them.
5.  You've got to go back to the same relationship.

In our human condition we make these mistakes regularly, but if we take the time to pray about our feelings, open ourselves up to God's leading, we can avoid them. Forgiveness doesn't have to mean rushing back into a damaging relationship or thinking that immoral behavior is okay once it's forgiven.

And, forgiving doesn't always mean forgetting. We carry with us the pain and sorrow of a broken relationship or hurtful behavior towards us. We just don't have to let it rule our lives.

Whom do you need to forgive? Think carefully about the feelings this person's name evokes. Who is paying the price for your lack of forgiveness? Remember, forgiveness isn't necessarily a feeling; it is an

---

[2]    Lewis B. Smedes, *The Art of Forgiving* (New York: Moorings, 1996), 23 – 36.

act — a conscious act based on what you know about forgiving and its cleansing power.

And, just as important as our forgiving others is our own need to seek forgiveness and humble ourselves before the Lord.

Forgiveness is a choice; don't let it pass you by.

Prayer: Dear Lord, help me to be forgiving even when the other person doesn't care. Amen.

Grace

*For it is by grace you have been saved, through faith – and this not from yourselves, it the gift of God – not by works, so that no one can boast.* (Ephesians 2: 8 & 9)

There are those who think we need to offer grace to everyone – friend and enemy, and that we must offer this grace to people who don't even know they need it. Some equate forgiveness and grace, often using them interchangeably. I agree that forgiveness is important, but I am also sure that we are only able to truly forgive if we have received God's grace. It is the only way to understand fully how asking for forgiveness from Jesus and receiving it places us in a state of grace.

It is the prerequisite to being able to forgive and mean it. How many times have you been hurt, and I mean really, deeply wounded by another person? Grace is the last thing you are thinking about when your pain is raw and fuels the anger you feel. When you take it to the Lord, are you demanding he listen to just your side of the story? Maybe you could offer your feelings as well as the other person's and ask him to remind <u>you</u> that his grace is for everyone if they seek it. Ask him to give you the strength to forgive and show that his grace is working in your life.

You are not required to offer grace from yourself; only God can do that. You can offer forgiveness and describe how you are able to forgive because of Christ's grace in you. It is a tall order. In our human condition we want revenge, hurt, unhappiness for those who abuse us. You set yourself apart when you are able to live a grace-filled life.

When I first became a Christian, I learned this acrostic:

<u>G</u>od's
<u>R</u>iches
<u>A</u>t
<u>C</u>hrist's
<u>E</u>xpense

We receive the riches of God's love and forgiveness because Christ gave his life on the cross. We are saved through grace, Jesus' ultimate sacrifice for each of us. I believe we are to forgive others so they know what the grace of Jesus Christ is really about. I don't think we actually offer **grace** to others; we are able to offer **forgiveness** because we live under the grace Jesus provided for us at the cross.

Whatever your understanding, both grace and forgiveness bring amazing relief! Think about those who have hurt you and those you have yet to forgive.

Ask Jesus specifically for the power to let it go.

Prayer: Lord, help me let go of hurts and broken promises so I can forgive openly and truthfully. Amen.

Sanctified or Sanctimonious?

*Now may the God of peace himself sanctify you completely, and may your whole spirit and soul and body be kept blameless at the coming of our Lord Jesus Christ.*

1Corinthians 1:2 *To the church of God that is in Corinth, to those sanctified in Christ Jesus, called to be saints together with all those who in every place call upon the name of our Lord Jesus Christ, both their Lord and ours* (2Thessalonians 5:23)

*So Jesus also suffered outside the gate in order to sanctify the people through his own blood.*

(Hebrews 13:12)

We visited our daughter and her family this weekend in their new home in Missouri. On Sunday we had the privilege of attending their new church home. The topic for the sermon was a portion of an ongoing series entitled "Beyond Normal". The subject was sex. The pastor told a funny story about putting the sermon title on the roadside bulletin board which read, "Beyond Normal: Sex". When he drove to work the next morning and saw the sign, he decided it wasn't exactly the message they were trying to send so they changed it to just "Beyond Normal."

I can't really tell you how the message conveyed a sense of stretching yourself beyond what you normally do; I think he wanted to tell us to turn away from the message of the world – if it feels good, do it – and turn back to the Biblical principles of morality. But, one thing he said caught my attention: are you sanctified or are you just sanctimonious? He didn't elaborate, but my brain took off in a whole new direction. (That's probably why I didn't get the point of his sermon.)

To sanctify is literally "to set apart for special use or purpose," figuratively "to make holy or sacred." As the scripture tells us, when we become Christians, we are set apart, achieving the righteousness of God without paying any penalty in order to receive it. We are sanctified (made holy, set apart for God's purpose) through Christ. It is a free gift.

But, too many times, we turn being sanctified into being sanctimonious: Making a show of being morally superior to other people. I have seen it happen over and over again: Declaring yourself a Christian, taking on a new life, and serving God turns into declaring yourself better than everyone else, taking on a life of hypocrisy, and serving yourself more than serving others. How does it happen?

Well, I think it happens slowly, insidiously, and unintentionally. We try to build ourselves up through good works while still clinging to the pleasures of this world. We relish the praise we get when we do something sacrificial for our church, and before we know it, we're slaving away on church projects in order to reap the ooohs and aaahs of the less capable. We crave recognition; we want to be special.

The truth is that we <u>are</u> special in the eyes of God. We are his. We shouldn't need anything else to make us feel set apart. Just believe that you are set apart for God's purposes. Unfortunately, that means we are to be set apart from this world, keeping our focus on things above and doing good works for the sheer pleasure of glorifying our Master. There is no room for self-aggrandizement.

Think about it – wouldn't you much rather hear "well done, good and faithful servant" from God than from your neighbor? Your boss? Or even your kids? Our world is full of false praise as well as false modesty.

So, answer the question for yourself: are you sanctified or sanctimonious? Or both????

Prayer: Lord, I want to be sanctified; help me in my need to be recognized. Amen.

All Hat and No Cattle

*For this is the message that you heard from the beginning that we should love one another, not as Cain who was of the wicked one and murdered his brother. And why did he murder him? Because his works were evil and his brother's righteous. We know that we have passed from death to life, because we love our brothers. He who does not love his brother abides in death.* (1John 2: 12 – 14)

There's a phrase in the southern regions of our country that goes, "Aww, he's all hat and no cattle." It means that he talks a good game but can't deliver on his promises. He's just talk.

How many times have you watched a politician blow about his/her solutions to our country's problems? They go on and on about their plans to bring about change – for the better. And, guess what? Nothing changes for the better, just more of the same or worse. Or more personally, one of your friends claims to have accepted Christ as Savior and talks about how he has changed and that his life will be all for Jesus. A few weeks later, you realize nothing has changed in your friend, and his talk was just that – talk.

The apostle John reminds us that anyone who proclaims the love of Christ must back it up with a basic behavior: love your brother, not because you think it will look good, but because you truly have the love of Christ in your heart and want to live and love as he requires. Only those who love their brothers can claim they have truly passed from death to life in Christ.

The bottom line is we can talk all we want about having Christ in our hearts, but when it comes to living the life that proves it… we're all hat and no cattle. Decide today that you will be different, that you will be the loving, caring, compassionate servant you have been called to be.

Real change, real life, real love.

Prayer: Lord, show me my brothers and their needs, and I will serve you through them. Amen.

What's in a Name?

*She will bear a Son; and you shall call His name Jesus, for He will save His people from their sins." Now all this took place to fulfill what was spoken by the Lord through the prophet:* [23] "BEHOLD, THE VIRGIN SHALL BE WITH CHILD AND SHALL BEAR A SON, AND THEY SHALL CALL HIS NAME [c]IMMANUEL," *which translated means,* "GOD WITH US.". (Matthew 1: 21 – 23)

When I first knew I was expecting a baby, the doctor gave me a little pink book that was all about what to expect from pregnancy. In the back was a list of baby names, and when I saw the name Evan, I knew that was the one I wanted for our son. We didn't know we were having a boy, but that didn't stop me from choosing his name. From that day on, the baby was Evan to me. It was a special name for a special new person who would make our lives infinitely more complex, yet filled with the simplicity of deep, abiding love. I never imagined I could love another human being as much as I love my son and my daughter, Erica. The sound of their names evokes a warm, wonderful feeling to this day.

It was the same for Mary and Joseph. She didn't find Jesus' name in a little pink pregnancy book; Joseph heard it straight from an angel of the Lord himself. So you may think that "Jesus" shouldn't have been his name if the Lord said to call him Immanuel (See Isaiah 7:14), but in ancient times, names were often chosen to show the purpose of a person's life. Jesus is synonymous with salvation, and Immanuel is synonymous with "God with us." Jesus came as God in the flesh to save us from our sins. So Jesus = God = Immanuel. In fact, Jesus was also known as Mighty Counselor, Everlasting Father, and the Prince of Peace – all descriptive of God's purposes for his Son.

The very birth of Jesus gave us a purpose also: to proclaim the Good News throughout the world. If each of us had told of the saving grace of Jesus Christ in just our little part of the world, and those who heard passed it on, everyone would have heard it by now.

When we commit to sharing Jesus, our lives will be infinitely more complex, but Jesus will fill us with a deep, abiding love – greater than we can imagine. Maybe we should take some time to exalt the name of Jesus who came to save us from our sins, to dwell among us as God, and to give his life as a ransom for many. Just tell one other person and ask him/her to do the same. The Good News will spread like wildfire!

What's in a name?

Eternity.

Prayer: I will remember your name, O Lord, and praise you throughout eternity. Amen.

Pretendering

*In the presence of God and of Christ Jesus, who will judge the living and the dead, and in view of his appearing and his kingdom, I give you this charge: ² Preach the word; be prepared in season and out of season; correct, rebuke and encourage—with great patience and careful instruction. ³ For the time will come when people will not put up with sound doctrine. Instead, to suit their own desires, they will gather around them a great number of teachers to say what their itching ears want to hear. ⁴ They will turn their ears away from the truth and turn aside to myths. ⁵ But you, keep your head in all situations, endure hardship, do the work of an evangelist, discharge all the duties of your ministry.* (2Timothy 4: 1- 5)

Our grandson, Fischer, spent the weekend with us, and we watched a lot of movies! One of his favorites is "Piglet's Big Movie." In one of the scenes, Tigger says, "Is he really lost, or is he just pretendering?" I love that word; the way he said it made me pay attention. And it got me to thinking about all the times in The Bible that Jesus warns us about "pretendering." Here are just a few:

"do not be like the hypocrites…" (Matthew 6:5)
"do not do what they do…" (Matthew 23)
"I thank you that I am not as other men are…" (Luke 18:11)
(Be sure to read around those verses, too, to get the context.)

So, the big question is: Are you pretendering? How sincere are you in your prayers, service, and speech as an example to others? Will you be one of those whose ears will itch? Will you turn away from the truth? Believe me, the time is coming when we will be tested in our faith. Look around you. The signs of oppression are there even though we cannot conceive of a time when we couldn't be open in our Christianity. And even if that persecution is not just around the corner, the words we say today and the heartfelt commitment we make to Jesus will surely influence those around us.

One of the worst stumbling blocks we place in front of non-believers is that of hypocrisy. People are so sensitive to insincerity – especially when it comes to Christians. One misspoken word, one unkind action can cancel out a lot of good deeds done for the right reasons. While we know that we cannot be perfect until the day of Jesus Christ, when his coming erases all evil, others don't necessarily know that. They only see us through the world view. So, be careful in your daily interactions. Live your life as a true representative of all the good Jesus has proclaimed.

Stop pretendering; it won't help you or anyone else.

Prayer: Lord, give me a sincere heart that helps me to love as you have loved. Amen.

You Can Only Cover Up So Much.

*Can anyone hide in secret places so that I cannot see him?" declares the LORD. "Do not I fill heaven and earth?" declares the LORD.* (Jeremiah 23:24)

My sister came over this weekend to re-cover a chair for our new bedroom. She always does such a good job on any project she undertakes. The sisters in my family have all benefited from her excellent skills. She removed about a zillion staples and carefully de-constructed the chair's cover so she could use it as a pattern for the new fabric. It was tedious and tiring work.

It reminded me of how God uncovers our sins. He peels back the facades we so carefully construct and shows us the truth about ourselves. He talks to us throughout this process with reassuring words and actions. He is always there to show us the secret places we try to hide from others and from him. But there is nowhere to hide. He sees all, knows all, uncovers all.

And then, when we are exposed before him, he reconstructs our hearts to be more like him. "When we confess our sins, he is faithful and just and will forgive us our sins and cleanse us from all unrighteousness." (I John 1:9) Just like recovering that chair, he puts on a new layer -- and we are new creatures in him. No hiding, no lying, no covering up. We don't have to.

We become beautiful in his sight -- and that is all that really matters.

Prayer: Lord, I stand before you today and ask that you uncover any sins I have ignored. Amen.

Words to Live By

*Only take care, and keep your soul diligently, lest you forget the things that your eyes have seen, and lest they depart from your heart all the days of your life. Make them known to your children and your children's children—* (Deuteronomy 4:9)

Five of our grandchildren are going to visit us this week. We miss them terribly now that they have moved away. But we are happy they love their new home and their new school and have found a church family. We, of course, only want the best for them - our own needs aside. For those of you who have grandchildren, this message will probably strike a chord of empathy. We all want to be a positive influence on our children and grandchildren and love having them near us. (Our other grandsons are only a few miles away.) But, thanks to the huge strides in technology, we can "skype" with our Missouri group and keep up with their lives on Facebook. Of course when Moses delivered this message to the Israelites, he had no idea we would be able to see our grandchildren with the click of a mouse.

Moses' message was a final reminder to the children of the desert years: do not forget where you came from, what the Lord has taught you, what you are called to be and do. They were just about to enter the Promised Land - the land flowing with milk and honey. And Moses knew he wouldn't be there to counsel them and keep them on the holy path. He had just spent 40 years with them and knew all too well their wanderings and missteps. He had made a few of his own, not the least of which was to anger God enough to deny him entry into this new land.

If you read the entire book of Deuteronomy, you will see that Moses covers just about every eventuality the Israelites will face: driving out nations, having one place of worship, eating of clean and unclean foods, canceling debts, worshipping other gods, setting up courts for the law, to name a few. And, throughout the entire book, Moses reviews how they are to love the Lord, fear him, worship him, and never forget him.

I encourage you to read the entire book of Deuteronomy. Read it as a commencement speech given to us as we embark on a new and exciting journey to love God more, to fear God more, and to live only for him. It's not a book to nitpick or worry over single verses -- you will only find yourself discouraged and confused. No, it is Moses' farewell speech -- he is giving his children and their children, and their children's children words to live by.

We must do the same with our knowledge of Jesus Christ - how our lives have been changed by his presence, how we have grown through his wisdom and what we can do in the future to carry this legacy forward to new generations.

We are blessed to have grandchildren, but we are also blessed to be able to share the Good News with them.

Christ gave his life for each one of us; repent of your sins and ask him to be the Lord of your life. Then tell your grandchildren.

Prayer: Lord, I confess my sins to you and ask that you come into my life. Amen.

Hakuna Matata

*For those who live according to the flesh set their minds on the things of the flesh, but those who live according to the Spirit set their minds on the things of the Spirit.* (Romans 8:5)

I listen with interest to the news commentaries and reports that encourage the tolerance of ungodly actions. We have created a culture where there is no absolute truth. Just live like you want. There is no reason to discriminate in your opinions; yours is as valid as mine. (I'm not using the negative for discriminate. I am using it as originally defined: to mark or perceive the distinguishing or peculiar features of). We argue endlessly about right and wrong. What is right for you may not be right for me.

Who's to say what is wrong?

Well, I'll tell you who says: God.

Let's just follow this logic to its natural conclusion. If we live according to the open, live-and-let-live, nothing-really-matters philosophy, the anything goes, if-it-feels-good, do-it plan, we will eventually have no regard for fellow humans. We will slide down that slippery slope of self-indulgence, the one that inevitably leads to getting what I want at any cost. We may think this statement is an exaggeration, but look back 20 years, and you will see what I mean. We already accept behavior that just a few years ago was considered not only unacceptable but illegal. In our effort to be nice and include everyone, to be completely non-judgmental, we ignore the warning signs of a declining society. The basic question is where does it end?

On the other hand, if we follow God's rules, if we live according to His Word, if we love our neighbors as ourselves, we honor life, give all we can to support each other, and find a way to resolve our differences that draws us closer to Him. We build a society (and hopefully a world) that grows and prospers -- not just for some but for all. You don't have to legislate it. In fact, you can't. You can only live to honor God by choice. He sent His Son to die for all of us. "If you confess with your mouth and believe in your heart that Jesus was raised from the dead, you will be saved." (Romans 10: 9, 10)

Our grandson loves the movie *The Lion King*. He can even recite some of the lines. At one point, the characters sing the phrase hakuna matata. They proclaim this new philosophy as the best way to live your life: No worries for the rest of your days. Wouldn't that be nice?

The only way to achieve that goal is to surrender to Jesus and promise to live according to His teachings.

The bottom line is when God makes the rules, and we follow them, we find peace. When man makes the rules, or worse, doesn't have any, we find chaos and ultimate demise as a society.

Think about it.

Prayer: Lord, I want to live for you and surrender my worries and worldly thoughts to you. Amen.

## Personal Prayer Partner

*If any of you lacks wisdom, let him ask God, who gives generously to all without reproach, and it will be given him.* (John 1:5)

Who else can you ask anything – anything at all – and never worry about reproach? We often preface our statements to others with, "I know this is a stupid question" or "Don't laugh…" We NEVER have to preface our prayers with those words. We must trust that God hears us, loves us, and will answer our pleas with the perfect response in his perfect time.

Hebrews 4:16 tells us: "Let us then approach God's throne of grace with confidence, so that we may receive mercy and find grace to help us in our time of need." We can go boldly before God and be assured he will offer mercy and grace. And, while we cannot always find a friend to listen to us without reproach or the hope of receiving mercy and grace, we can always find the Lord, ready and waiting – a willing prayer partner.

If you struggle with what to say, think about it in terms of talking to a trusted friend. Isn't there someone in your life to whom you can pour out your heart? What would you say to that friend? Would you worry about how you phrase things, how you plead your case? Probably not. It is exactly the same if you are talking to God. He doesn't really care how you say the words, just that you say them to him as your trusted friend who loves you and wants the best for you.

Cry out to him, if you need to. Praise him even if you are overwhelmed. Pour your heart out to him and know you are heard.

Prayer is a privilege, a special advantage that only we as followers of Jesus can experience. Don't over-think it; don't worry about getting it right.

Just do it.

Prayer: Lord, thank you for the privilege of prayer. Amen.

And Best of All…

*God is with you in everything you do.* (Genesis 21:22)

*The virgin will be with child and will give birth to a son, and they will call him "Immanuel" which means "God is with us."* (Matthew 1:23)

The last words of John Wesley were "And best of all, God is with me." He said these words twice and then passed away.

As you may know, John Wesley was the founder of Methodism, a sect of believers in England in the 1700's. His convictions about living the Christian life led him to teach others about the disciplines/ methods of prayer, study, and worship, and so they were called Methodists. He brought this form of discipline to the United States and began what we know today as the itinerant ministry of the United Methodist Church. John Wesley came here himself numerous times to encourage and teach others about the importance of disciplining ourselves in prayer and service to God.

But the real key is in knowing that John Wesley took God's promise to be with him as the truth of his life. He never wavered from his dedication to spreading the Gospel. He and his brother Charles wrote hundreds of hymns that are sung today – not just in Methodist churches but in many other Protestant congregations as well. Each one is a message in itself relating the pure love of Jesus and his unrelenting pursuit of our hearts to be won through salvation.

We can also be assured that God is with us. While he may seem far away at times, he is always as close as our uttered prayer. He promises never to leave, and that is enough.

I have been reading some postings on Facebook lately that challenge the existence of God. They support the ideas brought forth in

Stephen Hawking's new book, *The Grand Design.* I have only read some reviews and excerpts from this book, but he offers his theory of why there is no intelligent design in our universe. The postings refer to "religious people" as needing a crutch to stave off their fears, not being able to accept that this earth and this life is all there is. I have to tell you that I am overwhelmed by this way of thinking. I told the Lord that I am totally inadequate when it comes to understanding why these people feel the way they do. I am at a loss as to how to address their point of view.

But, then, I always go back to what my sister-in-law told me she says when confronted with this viewpoint: "If you're right and I'm wrong, I've still led a pretty good life, serving a God who I am convinced loves me and wants the best for me. But, if I'm right, and you're wrong, eternity is… well, eternity."

I'll say it again: don't let your need to prove your intellectual superiority get in the way of your salvation.

Prayer: Lord, please enter my trembling heart and allow me to feel Your unbounded love. Amen.

Pray for the Best, Hope for the Best; Do your Best.

*Be joyful always; pray continually; give thanks in all circumstances, for this is God's will for you in Christ Jesus.* (1Thessalonians 5:17)

These words were in Paul's final instructions to the church at Thessalonica. He also reminded them that they have hope in a Holy Spirit who knows their needs and will give them courage in the days to come. "Do not put out the Spirit's fire; do not treat prophecies with contempt. Test everything. Hold on to the good. Avoid every kind of evil." (1Thes 5:19 – 22)

As followers of Christ, we know that prayer is essential to enjoying our relationship with him. Pray **for** everything. Pray **about** everything. And, while you're at it, thank the Lord for the hope he provides you in eternal life. Remember who has given you the power to pray as well as the power to do your best.

Jesus expects us to work hard, giving thanks for our ability to think and act. We must grasp the weight of our responsibility in praying, hoping and working. While the Holy Spirit supports our efforts, it is up to us to seek his counsel, continue our hope for the best life, and work to achieve what we were called to be in this world.

Jesus could have called on an army of angels to rescue him from the devil's temptation; he could have called on his Father to relieve him of the weight of the cross; he must have been fed up with the apathy surrounding him as he tried to tell the people who he was, but did he give up on the mission he was sent to accomplish? No. He prayed, prayed, and then prayed more. He faced the cross with the hope of his return to paradise, and he taught, touched, and transformed those around him.

Can we do less? We can pray, hope, and work. And, we can do it all for the glory of God who loved us and gave his only Son that we might have eternal life.

The best is yet to come.

Prayer: Lord, remind me daily what a joy it is to pray to you. Amen.

Whom Do You Serve?

*But if serving the LORD seems undesirable to you, then choose for yourselves this day whom you will serve, whether the gods your forefathers served beyond the River, or the gods of the Amorites, in whose land you are living. But as for me and my household, we will serve the LORD.*

(Joshua 24:15)

We have a cross on the wall facing our front door. The last sentence in this verse is posted above it. Our hope is that anyone who enters will know that we try to live according to the Lord's commands in this house.

We didn't always care so much about what the Lord has to say — about anything. We lived our lives pretty much like everyone else we knew. We loved the things of this world without even realizing it. We thought we were doing pretty well, going along to get along, finding a balance between what we liked about serving the Lord and what we wanted from the bigger world view.

Then we experienced some problems — big ones. Our faith would become the cornerstone that held us together. We made a choice to focus on the Lord and his principles, giving up the things that called us to the darker, self-serving, worldly life we knew was wrong. It has required turning off the TV or at least changing the channel to something else. We have found a new fulfillment in reading books about how to live for God. We listen to cds and radio programs that remind us whom we serve.

I had always thought the Lord was first in my life and that he was there for me in every situation. Well, the last part is right. I realized how much I had ignored his call to live for him and him alone. I am trying to set aside the things that call me from my determination to know him better. I <u>want</u> to know him better, serve him better.

Here are some of the actions I now take – diligently, not just when I have time:

1. Reading the Bible. I don't see it as a chore any longer or something I have to do. I look forward to it as a way to end my day on a high note and introduce me to a time of prayer.
2. Praying. I used to fit prayers in around the activities of my day. Now, it is the activity of my day. It is the seal I put on my day – a final conversation with the One I love.
3. Learning. I try to learn a verse or a concept each day – one I can apply to my life at that moment. For example, "I keep my eyes on the Lord always for he is the only one who can free my feet from the snare." *(Psalm 25:15)*
4. Doing. I am no longer worried about what people think. My only judge is Christ, and I want to please him in all I do.

Whom will you serve? Decide today to serve the One who made you, loves you, and cares for you.

Prayer: Lord, I want to serve you today, and every day. Amen.

Persistence

*And ye shall be hated of all men for my name's sake: but he that shall persist unto the end, the same shall be saved.* (Mark 13:13 King James)

How many of you would call yourselves persistent? Tenacious? Dog-with-a-bone? I think there are certain things we are all persistent about. I find myself being "dog-with-a-bone" persistent about solving some issues I am have with our health care administration. In fact, I have been persistent for the past seven years. And why am I so set on getting this issue solved? Money. If they don't pay me what I am owed, I will continue to call and write letters until they do.

If you want to know what is really important to people, follow their money. If you want to know what is important to an organization, follow their money. We hate to admit it, but it is a fact of our culture. We have made money a priority. There is a danger in making things or people our idols. We worry way too much about it.

"Seek ye first the kingdom of God and his righteousness, and all these things will be added to you." *(*Matthew 6:33) We don't have to worry about money or things. God provides for our needs. Note I said our needs, not our wants.

But, in all practicality, how do we curb our desire for more things, more money, more wants?

Prayer.

Combined with a sincere persistence to know the Word of God, prayer is undeniably the best way to ward off these concerns. Put God first, seeking his righteousness through a commitment to Jesus Christ. Confess your shortcomings; pledge to follow His path. Read your Bible.

Am I repeating myself? Yes I am. We don't hear it enough. The Lord has given us a complete set of instructions for living life to the fullest. What more do we need? Apparently, a lot if you check the number of translations, biblical reference books, interpretations, and commentaries. But I am talking about the pure Word of God.

I am a firm believer that God knows the translation in my lap. He can speak to me in the 21st century because "he knows the beginning and the end of time" (Isaiah 46:10). He always knows who I am and what I need. When I seek Him in his Word, he will lead me through it.

Seek God in his Word, and know he will bless your efforts. Be persistent and dig deep into his treasures!

Pray!

You won't be disappointed.

Prayer: Lord, remind me to seek You first. Amen.

God's Phone Number

*Call to me and I will answer you...* (Jeremiah 33:3)

There is so much I could say about prayer. It is, of course, our open communication line with Jesus. It has become an important part of my life, and I highly recommend it as a way to ease pain, find encouragement, unload, and draw near to the Lord.

Do you find yourself going to the Lord in prayer with a laundry list of complaints and requests? I often start out strong only to slip into the old pattern of giving God instructions on how he should run my life. Sort of misses the point, huh?

And, I'm not new to a prayer life. I learned to pray early in my Christian walk from some very devout women who weren't afraid to be bold before the throne. But I still find myself craving a true intimacy in my prayer time. Does God really hear me? Or, am I just another voice droning on about how big my problems are? He is probably listening and thinking, oh, you think you've got problems; don't even go there with me. I'll show you problems...

The truth is there are some requirements for God to hear us.

1. You must come to him with a contrite heart, truly confessing your sins and being resolved to correct them. (Psalm 51)
2. You cannot be holding onto resentment or mistrust for a brother/sister. (Matthew 5:24)
3. Pray for God's will to be done, not your own. (Matthew 6:10)
4. Approach your prayers with humility. (Matthew 6:5)
5. Be thankful. (1 Thessalonians 5:16-18).

Be what? There are times when I am not thankful at all. I am angry, frustrated, hurt, desperate and lost. But, the Lord is still there, and he's brought a friend. "In the same way, the Spirit helps us in our weakness. We do not know what we ought to pray for, but the Spirit himself intercedes for us with groans that words cannot express." (Romans 8:26) When you are hurting so bad that you don't even know what to pray, the Holy Spirit is there to do it for you.

Prayer is what makes God personal. He longs to talk with us, be in our lives, comfort us, and guide us. When I was young in the faith, my friend Sandy encouraged me to use a formula prayer to get started. Using the word ACTS as a guide, just talk to the Lord:

A – Adoration
C – Confession
T – Thanksgiving
S – Supplication

So, dial Him up; he's waiting to hear from you.

Prayer: Lord, I know I can call on you anytime and you will answer. Help me remember your promises. Amen.

A Little Word with HUGE Meaning…

*And forgive us our sins as we forgive those who sin against us.* (Matthew 6: 12)

When I first learned what the Lord's Prayer was really about, I was astonished to find that the interpretation of verse twelve meant God forgives us just like we forgive others. What??

Of course I had learned the prayer as a child, but I didn't really dig into it until I was teaching Vacation Bible School one year to third graders. We broke down the prayer verse by verse to show how personal it is for all of us, not just grownups. I wanted them to see this prayer isn't just some words from the Bible but a call to each of us to live and serve God as he said, not how we want.

I read several versions of the Lord's Prayer in preparation for the class, and of course, each used sins, debts, trespasses interchangeably. But the word that struck me with a new force was the little word "as." I thought it meant "along with us," not "like." I was sure my God was right there forgiving these others just as I was doing, but that is not the relationship God was talking about. He is telling me to forgive others just as I hope he will forgive me, and if I'm holding out on my forgiveness of someone else, he will withhold **his** forgiveness of me. Uh-oh. That little word revealed a whole new responsibility on my part.

Not only am I called to forgive, but I am also reminded of a just God who will hold me to it. Now I have some skin in the game. Now I know the importance of truly living a life that affords the same grace to others as God has given me. Think about real forgiveness – how we forgive others for our own peace even if the other party doesn't care he/she has received it – but this element of the Lord's Prayer takes it one step farther. Our own forgiveness – not someone else's – relies on our truthfully saying those words: Please, Lord, forgive me just as I have forgiven those who have hurt/lied about/forgotten about/ignored me.

It's a simple prayer with powerful meaning. The next time you recite it, think about what you are really saying. You don't want to miss a single word.

Prayer: Lord, help me to have a forgiving heart and an understanding ear to others. Amen.

Alphabet of Praise

*I will extol the Lord at all times; his praise will always be on my lips. My soul will boast in the Lord; let the afflicted rejoice. Glorify the Lord with me; let us exalt his name together.* (Psalm 34:1-3)

Sometimes during my prayer time, I find myself drifting. Has that ever happened to you? To get myself back on track I do a mental exercise I hope shows the Lord how much I love him and want to worship him at all times.

I start with A and go to Z, naming something that praises the Lord. Here is an example:

A – Adoration
B – Blessed
C – Comforter
D – Divine
E – Eternal

You get the idea. The letter X takes some imagination but I just use an "X" sound. I'm sure the Lord doesn't mind, the Xalted one, most Xcellent God.

He has called us to be his children, and we should be forever grateful. What does it take to focus on the Father? Just a word of praise ready and waiting on your lips. When you have a down moment, use it to send up a praise. You will soon find your thoughts will turn more positive; you won't complain as much; you start to see the good around you instead of the problems.

When I wake up in the middle of the night, my alphabet game works really well to calm me down so I can get back to sleep. It keeps me from worrying and chasing my troubles around in my head. I am able to move myself more towards "being thankful in all my circumstances."

Here is the rest of Psalm 34. It is a wonderful model for praise and worship -- just between you and God.

**Of David. When he pretended to be insane before Abimelek, who drove him away, and he left.**

¹ "I will extol the LORD at all times;

> his praise will always be on my lips.

² I will glory in the LORD;

> let the afflicted hear and rejoice.

³ Glorify the LORD with me;

> let us exalt his name together.

⁴ I sought the LORD, and he answered me;

> he delivered me from all my fears.

⁵ Those who look to him are radiant;

> their faces are never covered with shame.

⁶ This poor man called, and the LORD heard him;

> he saved him out of all his troubles.

⁷ The angel of the LORD encamps around those who fear him,

and he delivers them.

⁸ Taste and see that the LORD is good;

blessed is the one who takes refuge in him.

⁹ Fear the LORD, you his holy people,

for those who fear him lack nothing.

¹⁰ The lions may grow weak and hungry,

but those who seek the LORD lack no good thing.

¹¹ Come, my children, listen to me;

I will teach you the fear of the LORD.

¹² Whoever of you loves life

and desires to see many good days,

¹³ keep your tongue from evil

and your lips from telling lies.

¹⁴ Turn from evil and do good;

seek peace and pursue it.

¹⁵ The eyes of the LORD are on the righteous,

and his ears are attentive to their cry;

¹⁶ but the face of the LORD is against those who do evil,

to blot out their name from the earth.

<sup>17</sup> The righteous cry out, and the LORD hears them;

he delivers them from all their troubles.

<sup>18</sup> The LORD is close to the brokenhearted

and saves those who are crushed in spirit.

<sup>19</sup> The righteous person may have many troubles,

but the LORD delivers him from them all;

<sup>20</sup> he protects all his bones,

not one of them will be broken.

<sup>21</sup> Evil will slay the wicked;

the foes of the righteous will be condemned.

<sup>22</sup> The LORD will rescue his servants;

no one who takes refuge in him will be condemned."

Prayer: Dearest Lord, I adore you and give you all the praise and glory in my life. Amen.

New Beginnings

*Therefore, if anyone is in Christ, he is a new creation; the old has gone, the new has come!* (2Corinthians 5:17)

Let's think about the first step in a new journey. We can beat ourselves up over the past, and we can wallow in our regrets, but even better, we can start a new journey with a new attitude. There is a saying that goes: The past is gone, the future is a mystery, the present is all we have.

I find myself reliving sad moments – not just from this past year but years in the past. I think if I rework them in my mind, I can feel better about how poorly I handled them. What nonsense. The past is the past – period. I can't change a thing about it. I can only resolve to do better in the future. But clichés won't help when you are in the depths of despair about what you could have done differently.

So let's just get them out of the way and move on:

I could have said…
I wish I had done…
I wish I hadn't done…
I couldn't help it…
It wasn't my fault… (maybe it was)
I wish I could take it back…
I should have…

The fact is there is nothing to say. Whatever you are grieving is done, and while you may still grieve, you cannot continue to try to explain your pain or ease your pain with "what if's". I am so trapped in this idea of "fixing it" that I can't see the futility of it. There is no fixing it; there is no making it easier. Time is the only thing that will really help, time and a resolution to live in the present. You can learn from the past, and your choices today will undeniably affect the future. But longing for the past or worrying about the future is a total waste of time.

I hold fast to the commitment of a life lived for Jesus Christ. He is the only one who can help me live in the present, learn from the past and trust in the future. The first step in your journey has to be to live a new life in Christ. Remember Galatians 2:20: "I have been crucified with Christ and I no longer live, but Christ lives in me. The life I live in the body, I live by faith in the Son of God, who loved me and gave himself for me."

I have recently had another lesson in giving up my pain to the Lord. When I cry out to him to hear my prayers of grief, even if he doesn't answer right away, I feel a little better. The pain is shared, and I know he still wants the best for me and my best for him.

It's a start.

Prayer: Lord, start me on the road to new life in you. I am ready to take the first step. Amen.

Breaking Free

*Let them give thanks to the LORD for his unfailing love and his wonderful deeds for mankind, [16] for he breaks down gates of bronze and cuts through bars of iron.* (Psalm 107: 15&16)

*Be at rest once more, O my soul, for the LORD has been good to you.* (Psalm 116:7)

I get a lot of comfort reading the Psalms. No matter what state you are in, the Psalms will offer a way to either accept or, at the very least, understand why you are feeling the way you do. Sometimes, it's euphoria; sometimes it's despair. Either way, there are words in the Psalms to help you express your feelings.

We tend to build our own barriers to God's love. Picture yourself inside an iron cage. Name each of the bars that surround you: fear, apathy, jealousy, pain, gossip, impatience, guilt, addiction, unforgiven deeds, worldly possessions, love of money, despair. The list is as long as there are people reading this message. And the tighter you hold on, the thicker the bars and the more difficult they will be to break. We are mostly helpless to rid ourselves of these suffocating, ever encroaching bars. We may escape for a little while, but the door slams shut on us each time we add another barrier; it's almost as if we are clamoring to get in, not get out.

The good news is that nothing can stop the love of God -- no matter how many gates we close, walls we build or bars we shield ourselves with. He alone can break through. "You, dear children, are from God and have overcome them, because the one who is in you is greater than the one who is in the world." (1John 4:4) As long as we know we are HIS, we know there is nothing in this world that can overcome his love for us. We have the daily assurance that God loves us, and we can face the day knowing his power and grace surround us.

Now picture yourself praying down each bar on your cage. One by one God dismantles those barriers that hold you back. And you are free.

Prayer:

The sun comes up in the morning.
The moon comes up at night.
Never fear; God is near.
His love is a shining light. Amen.

Fear not…

*No one will be able to stand against you all the days of your life. As I was with Moses, so I will be with you; I will never leave you nor forsake you.* (Joshua 1:5)

I feel very blessed. I have everything I need and most of what I want. I love the Lord with all my heart, soul, mind and strength. I try to live every day for Him. So, what's the problem, you ask? I still live in fear; fear of loss, fear of tragedy, fear of doing or saying something wrong (Sadly, I still have perfectionist tendencies.), fear of the unknown. It is nipping at my heels like a yappy little dog who wants my constant attention. And, surely you can see that it's not my fault…

Our human condition drags us into the world of fear and mistrust, and our human experience confirms that bad things happen to good people. But more than 100 times in The Bible, God says "fear not". From Genesis to Revelation, God commands, "do not be afraid." He leads Old Testament people into battle with the promise of victory, but they still advance with timidity and fear. He rescues his people from starvation and slavery, but they defy his orders in fear of losing their worldly ways.

And here we are thousands of years later still trying to fight his loving care and promise of hope. And, of course, the more you fear, the more you fear. Where does it end?

It ends with the promise of God: "I will never leave you nor forsake you. Be strong and courageous. Do not be afraid or terrified because of them, for the LORD your God goes with you; he will never leave you nor forsake you." (Deuteronomy 31:6) He repeats his promise in Joshua 1:5 and again in Hebrews 13:5. How can we be afraid when we have the awesome God of the universe holding our hands? He is bigger than any fear we harbor; he is stronger than any tragedy; he is fully capable of making something we can't even imagine out of our pain.

Prayer: Lord, help me be ready for the stampede and trust you with my fears. Amen.

*Catherine J. Bowen*

## The Infinite, Infallible Word of God

*All Scripture is God-breathed and is useful for teaching, rebuking, correcting and training in righteousness, so that the servant of God may be thoroughly equipped for every good work.* (2 Timothy 3:16 – 17)

There are so many ways to look at God's word. In fact, the depths of his Holy Word are infinite. Just think about a few of the verses you have read or even just heard someone else talk about. There are as many meaningful experiences with a passage as there are people who have read it. I'm not talking about the exegesis (the extraction of the meaning of scripture; i.e., its explanation) of the Word but the real life, experiential impact of a particular scripture passage.

For example, one of the first verses I learned as a new Christian is I John 1:9: "If we confess our sins, he is faithful and just and will forgive us our sins and cleanse us from all unrighteousness." That verse is packed with wonderful promises from our God, whom I was just getting to know. It was wonderful to learn from the very beginning of my journey the importance of confession. It is cleansing, powerful, releasing, and comforting. I also began to build an unerring trust in the Lord who is faithful and just. He promises to forgive me when I come contrite, honestly seeking forgiveness. He NEVER turns anyone away. And there are volumes already written on how faithful and just God is.

As I grew in my faith, I also learned to accept the truth of God's Word as a whole. I don't try to justify it or make excuses for why I believe it. I don't try to defend the verses or passages that are hotbeds of disagreement, especially with my non-Christian friends. I don't cherry-pick the verses I like, and I don't dismiss the ones that are hard to accept. I have opened the Bible to a random page and found comfort in the first verse my eyes fell upon. I have also searched the

Scriptures diligently, looking for a passage th.
problems. It's all there, waiting to be discovered

Do you see the common denominator here? It isn't ju
the page; it is the heart of the person who is searching.
Word to speak to us where we are – joyful, hurting, hung.
lost and found. Once you have accepted Christ as your Sav.
Word will hold new and exciting depths of knowledge, revealii
you all the Lord has to give in your new life. Accept it or… reject ..

God's Word stands on its own merits – infinite and infallible.

Prayer: Lord, give me the strength to trust your Word, always and
forever. Amen.

*I Am a Dirt Sandwich*

speaks to my current

the words on

d uses his

thirsty,

the

o

*e mighty hand of God, that He*
*g all your anxiety upon Him,*

n 2002. It had been a tough
ather and continuing with
graduated from college,
ok on added and stressful
gave in and started taking medication. I
...nt to take it; I thought it was a sign of weakness and lack of trust in the Lord. But, the truth is, I am grateful for scientific advances that eased my pain and continue to help me stay ahead of the dark demons that have haunted me for so long.

I still have times when I feel myself slipping down into that black hole. The past week has been one of them. It takes all my energy to drag myself out of bed, focus on tasks that are really not that difficult and find ways to build myself back up. Prayer helps tremendously. I am comforted by the verses such as the one in I Peter. If God cares for me, he will take care of the fears that accompany my depression and "exalt me at the proper time." I don't have to face them by myself.

I think about the times my mother faced similar challenges. So many times I wanted to shake her and say, "Snap out of it! You have so much to be happy about." Ah, but now I understand. The feelings are complex and not so easily dismissed. I'm truly sorry, Mom.

We are all "fearfully and wonderfully made," even if imperfectly. I accept the dark times just as I accept the lighter times as part of living in an upside down world. My acceptance is a gift from God who knows my every thought before I think it and my every move before I make it. He will always provide a way out of the darkness if I am willing to see it.

His grace is always there.

Prayer: Thank you, Lord, for your grace. Amen.

*Catherine J. Bowen*

## Changing God???

*Let us then approach the throne of grace with confidence, so that we may receive mercy and find grace to help us in our time of need.* (Hebrews 4:16)

Do you think you can change the mind of God through prayer? It's a tough question, and I don't have the total answer. It has been argued since prayer began. The one thing I do know for certain is that God hears our prayers and wants to be in constant communication with us. I don't pray to change God's mind; I pray to draw closer to the One who knows the end from the beginning and can do ANYTHING.

I pray to strengthen my sense of God's presence in my life – a presence I will need to rely on no matter what the outcome of my prayers. I pray to find relief and peace in a world that doesn't make sense.

I am sure all of us have experienced the disappointment of prayers that seem to go unanswered. I prayed over and over for my brother's cancer to be cured, but it wasn't. I prayed that my friend, Sandy, would be cured, but she wasn't. I prayed that I would be cured, and I was.

How do we make sense of such seemingly random answers? If the Lord were answering prayers based on merit, they both deserved to be at the front of the line. I couldn't possibly measure up to their level of faithfulness. For whatever reason (which I will someday know and understand), through my healing, my faith was strengthened, my resolve to witness intensified, and my gratitude is unending.

I have to say the same regarding the fact that my prayers for them weren't answered in the way I hoped. Going through those experiences of loss made me stronger and drove me to my knees where I could feel God's love and compassion in the right measure.

So, we can pray, putting aside the question of changing God's mind. We can approach the throne with confidence and just be in his presence, just tell him what's on our minds, just accept whatever he has to say on the matter.

Spill your guts; you won't find a better listener.

Prayer: Hear me, O Lord, I need your listening ear. Amen.

Everyone I Know…

*And said unto him, Hearest thou what these say? And Jesus saith unto them, Yea; have ye never read, Out of the mouth of babes and sucklings thou hast perfected praise?* (Matthew 21:16, King James)

The chief priests and scribes (remember, they are the know-it-alls of the time.) are complaining about Jesus' attention to the blind, lame and the children crying out "Hosanna to the Son of David". And Jesus replies that surely they remember hearing this phrase about "out of the mouths of babes". And then he leaves them. No reprimand, no argument. There it is, fellas; take it or leave it. It's the truth. These little ones are pure of heart, and they have perfected praise – to the King of Kings.

When our grandson, Daniel, visited us a while ago, he asked me to pray with him at bed time. I was very happy to oblige. I knelt next to his bed, and he said a wonderful prayer that he had clearly memorized. Note that he was four years old at the time. While I couldn't understand every word, <u>he</u> definitely knew what he was talking about. I did hear one phrase that made me catch my breath: "God bless everyone I know, and everyone I don't know." Well, that just about covers it, doesn't it?

Ahh, out of the mouths of babes indeed. Can there be anything purer or sweeter than a little one who is praising the Lord? I found out later that this prayer is one that Daniel's brother Jonas made up for them to say at night before they go to sleep. Jonas was a wise old man of seven. And they are joined in this nightly ritual by their brother Aidan who was eight. What a memory they will have of ending each day saying this beautiful tribute to God, their family and their lives – and everyone else, apparently. Somebody is doing something right with these little guys (Mom and Dad)! I only wish I were there each night to witness it; what a joy.

And, note that Jonas didn't stop with "everyone I know." He wasn't going to take a chance on leaving anyone out of God's blessing, just in case they needed it.

We all need it.

Prayer: Lord, bless everyone I know, and everyone I don't know. Amen.

Little Changes Can Make a Big Difference

*You were taught, with regard to your former way of life, to put off your old self, which is being corrupted by its deceitful desires; to be made new in the attitude of your minds; and to put on the new self, created to be like God in true righteousness and holiness.* (Ephesians 4: 22 – 24)

Our daughter, Erica, was small for her age, and she got pretty tired of looking like a second grader when she was really in fifth grade. Arriving at church in her new Christmas dress, we were surprised that she refused to take off her coat. She clung tightly to the zipper as we tried to tell her she would be too warm. Finally, we gave up and took our seats. As the children gathered on the steps of the altar for the children's sermon, I could clearly see the problem. Another girl, a second-grader, was wearing the same dress. I understood completely.

After the service, her dad took her into the little room off the sanctuary and performed a miracle of change: he used the tiny scissors on his ever-present pocket knife to remove the satin rose and sash from her dress, and voilà -- she had a new dress. She happily bounced off to Sunday School, transformed back into a grown up fifth grader!

We can also make little changes to our lives that can make a big difference. In this passage from Ephesians, Paul is speaking to those believers who have committed their lives to Christ and are trying to live a new life in Him. While we are changed from sinner to saved when we accept Christ as Savior, we still need to make changes in our daily lives. Putting off our former way of life is difficult to say the least, but it can be accomplished with small changes stacked up to build a life of righteousness and holiness as God works in us.

What are the "deceitful desires" you are holding onto? How will you ever put off your old self if you continue to do the same corrupting things? Ask God to examine your life and your heart. Pray for insight into what you hold dear -- good and bad. Make a plan to change a little each day, putting on your new self, your new attitude, your new life in Christ.

You will be amazed at the difference.

Prayer: Search me, O Lord, and reveal to me the changes I need to make. Amen.

Disobedience=Judgment=Punishment/Forgiveness

*By the multitude of your iniquities, in the unrighteousness of your trade you profaned your sanctuaries; so I brought fire out from your midst; it consumed you, and I turned you to ashes on the earth in the sight of all who saw you.* (Ezekiel 28:18)

Our church has challenged each of us to read through the Bible in a year, and I am currently trudging through Leviticus. After the trials and tribulations of Genesis and Exodus, I can kind of understand why God laid out all the rules so diligently in Leviticus: These people don't get it! God has seen them through so much already; he has guided them out of Egypt, given them Moses as a trusted leader, told them over and over what he expects of them – and, more importantly – what will happen to them if they disobey. DO THEY LISTEN AND OBEY?????

NO.

They are more than willing to take their chances with a God who has proven to be a towering example of power, justice, and judgment. Think Pharaoh and the plagues. Think parting of the Red Sea. Think Passover. Do we need more examples?

Apparently we do. We are no different than the struggling, disobedient, arrogant, and sometimes evil Israelites. We go our own ways. We listen to what our neighbors say, rather than what God's Word says. We dismiss God's promise to separate the wheat from the chaff and throw the waste into the eternal fire (Revelation 14). We think we can get away with our living for nothing more than pleasure and gain. We neither listen nor obey.

So what? He forgave his chosen people many times over. But final judgment is coming for all of us. The difference now is we can live under the grace of Jesus Christ. We can experience eternal life with him. There are no more equations to be solved.

It is simple:

Disobedience=Judgment=Eternal Punishment
OR
Disobedience=Judgment =Eternal Forgiveness/Life

Do the math.

Prayer: Lord, I put my whole trust in you. You are my only hope. Amen.

## Filthy Rags to God's Riches

*All of us have become like one who is unclean, and all our righteous acts are like filthy rags; we all shrivel up like a leaf, and like the wind our sins sweep us away.* (Isaiah 64:6)

What do you feel like when you know you have sinned? Do you acknowledge what you have done as sin, or do you rationalize it as having a bad day, being drawn into wrongdoing by someone else, or ignoring it all together? I'm fairly sure you don't see yourself as donning the filthy rags of sin and guilt. And what about the times you think you've done something extraordinary? Feeling pretty good about yourself, right?

I hate to be the one to tell you, but only God is righteous by himself. He doesn't rely on anyone to declare his goodness or his holiness. And we can't declare our good deeds as righteous any more than we can declare that our sin doesn't matter. Our righteousness and the forgiveness of our sins go hand in hand with how much we love God and trust him to make us whole through Jesus Christ.

I love this passage from Isaiah. The word pictures are so vivid. I really can see myself shriveling up, blowing around recklessly and getting carried away with my own desires. There are so many ways to look at these few words:

Like one who is unclean – in ancient times, being unclean was one of the worst sins you could commit. Lepers were outcasts because they were the extreme of unclean. Priests were considered unclean if they didn't follow all of the rules laid out in the book of Leviticus, and only the right sacrifice to God would make them clean again. Today, we don't see ourselves as unclean unless we don't wash for a few days. We have lost our ability to "feel and see" our sin.

All our righteous acts are like filthy rags – not some but <u>all</u>. Think about the last thing you did that made you feel righteous. Was it pointing out someone else's inferiority? Was it winning a game because you thought you outsmarted an opponent? Was it a decision that went in your favor at work? Let me tell you how God sees those acts. They are nothing to him. In fact, they are worse than nothing; they are a pile of dirty, stinking rags. There is nothing humans can do to live up to the holy standard of God. He gave us rules; we broke them. He gave us second, third, fourth… tenth chances; we laughed and made idols for ourselves. He destroyed everything, and still we came back to mock and disobey him. Filthy, disgusting, self-absorbed sinners who only see the power of ourselves.

We all shrivel up like a leaf, and like the wind our sins sweep us away – I'm sure you have seen leaves in the Fall that are dried up. They blow easily, skittering across the ground with no power to stop themselves, no way to reclaim their green beauty. When we give in to sin, we are often blown about with no power to stop ourselves or regain what we have lost.

But, unlike the people of ancient times, we have hope. We can cast off the filthy rags of sin and guilt just by calling on the name of Jesus. He is able to make us righteous in God's eyes because he gave his life on the Cross. We can't earn righteousness; we can't buy God's favor; we can't bargain for another chance. We can only surrender our sin and claim the love of Jesus.

Filthy rags to God's riches. Every time.

Prayer: I give you my filthy rags, Lord, and wait upon your will. Amen.

Old News

*What has been will be again, what has been done will be done again; there is nothing new under the sun.* (Ecclesiastes 1:9)

I heard a quote the other day: new news is just old news told to new people. Solomon, the writer of Ecclesiastes, was one of the wisest men in the world. God gave him the power to discern the best solution to any problem. He gave Solomon this power because Solomon asked for it. God was impressed by Solomon's compassion and his longing for doing what is right.

In Ecclesiastes, Solomon has decided to try everything that will possibly bring him pleasure. He spares no expense and doesn't miss an opportunity to wallow in self-indulgence. And his conclusion? There is nothing new under the sun. It's all been done and will be done again. If Solomon were looking for a new high, a new discovery that would satisfy his longing for excitement, a new level of depravity, he was surely disappointed.

We tend to do the same thing. It's about the I'll-be-happy-when syndrome. We're all chasing some dream that will make us happier than we have ever been. Well, I hate to burst your bubble, but there is nothing out there that someone (several someones actually) hasn't already tried and found lacking; not money, sex, food, fame, jobs, relationships, or anything else you can think of.

Ecclesiastes 12 begins with *Remember your Creator.* God is the only one who fulfills. He is the only one who teaches us what is really important. He is the only one who will pass final judgment. This life on earth holds nothing new. Our human condition drives us into the wilderness of this world to search for something that will ultimately satisfy us. It isn't there.

Think about the verse above. We are bombarded with movies, television programs, and magazines that attempt to normalize what God has deemed wrong. The good guys don't always win the battle of good and evil any longer. We think of our society as being enlightened because we have accepted and defended sins. We justify the actions of others by blaming someone or something else – he had a bad childhood; she didn't mean for it to go that far; he doesn't remember what happened.

Study your history; it's all been done before. Previous cultures just called it by other names. And just as Solomon sought the wisdom of God to understand the disappointment and pain of turning to a sinful life, we must surrender our sinful life as well. *Don't be fooled. God is not mocked. You will surely reap what you sow* (Galatians 6:7). The very things you think are important today will fade, and you will be left with the consequences of your choices.

The best news of all is that you can receive forgiveness. "For all have sinned and fall short of the glory of God, but grace is the free gift of God in Jesus Christ." (Romans 3:23)

Tell this old news to new people.

Prayer: Lord, I will shout the Good News to everyone and pray for this fallen world. Amen.

Rainy Days and Mondays

Matthew 27: 62 – 28:20 Read the story of the guard at the tomb, Mary Magdalene and Mary seeing the stone rolled away, and Jesus appearing to them.

Easter Monday

So, now that Christ has risen from the dead, what next? The scriptures tell us that Jesus appeared not just to the Marys and the disciples but also to many others over the course of the next 40 days. These accounts are not fictional but substantiated by historical accounts as well. You can research historical evidence of the resurrection and find many sources. The basic evidence confirms that Jesus was crucified, buried in a tomb where a heavy stone was placed at the entrance. He rose from the grave and appeared to many people. The book of Acts gives the account of his ascension into heaven and the Holy Spirit moving among the crowd gathered as witnesses.

But what does all that mean to you and me? It means that we can speak boldly about the risen Christ. We don't have to hang our heads and mumble about what we celebrate on Easter or any day after. We KNOW Christ was raised from the dead. We BELIEVE he died for us just as he said he would. Read again the accounts of Jesus' ministry in Matthew, Mark, Luke and John. Jesus maintains his message throughout his time on earth: I came to save the lost.

Our pastor tells the story of a man in one of his early congregations who experienced his first Easter. Up to that point this man had just been going through the motions on Easter Sunday. But, his life changed when he accepted Christ as his Savior, and this Easter was the first one that meant something special to him. He had met the risen Lord; he understood the pain and suffering Jesus endured by taking on the sin of the world. Most of all he understood the resurrection – the cornerstone of our faith. Without it, Jesus would be just another nut claiming to be the long-awaited Messiah. But, he rose from the dead and ascended into heaven to sit at the right hand of God the Father. Death was defeated!

I remember my first Easter. I became a Christian on March 15, 1979, and Easter was just a few weeks after. I had always gone to church on Easter; it was a great excuse to buy a new dress. But this particular Easter morning was marked with joy, real joy knowing I would live forever in the presence of God, his Son and the Holy Spirit. I can't describe to you the change in my perspective; words are inadequate.

Have you experienced your first Easter? It is the ultimate celebration of life – eternal life.

Prayer: Lord, may every day be Easter Monday in my heart. Amen.

I'm God, and You're Not.

*Be still and know that I am God.* (Psalm 46:10)

Some of you will remember the Saturday Night Live newscast where Chevy Chase says, "I'm Chevy Chase, and you're not." A simple statement and really funny. It was all in the delivery, of course. He had a way of looking at the camera with a dead pan expression and saying the most outrageous things.

You know, God is saying the same thing in Psalm 46. (Read it for yourself.) He is reminding us that he is the only God. He holds the past and the future. He is sovereign, holy, and unyielding as a fortress. He shares the spotlight with no one! This Psalm also contains a verse that has helped me too many times to count. *God is our refuge and strength, an ever present help in trouble* (v. 1). When my life feels out of control, I remember this verse and feel some measure of peace – and more than that, hope.

I love the fact that God is calling me over the busyness of my life. He says, be still. Just be still; stop fussing, stop listing all of your problems and expectations. Just be still. You will be amazed how the enormity of his presence can be felt when you concentrate on the fact that he is God. Try to cut out all other distractions and just picture his face, his loving arms, his holiness.

Feel better? I always do. God is here. I have nothing to fear; he promised. Sounds easy enough. But what about all of those problems I have? What about my grief? What about my hurt feelings? What about my feeling like a total failure? I would love to tell you they all just go away if only you believe they will. Can't do it. The problems and pain are still there; I still feel them. The difference is that I also feel the assurance of a God who is...

Because he is, I can hold onto hope, push back fear, face another day. The world around me aches with loss, fights for position, disappoints all who rely on its "promises". But we can have peace in the knowledge that we don't have to remain in the world. God has conquered the world.

He already knows our problems, fears, joys, and mistakes. His hand is on the wheel, and he watches over us, shares our pain, and gives us comfort. He can intervene or be there to pick up the pieces of our broken lives. Nothing can change that fact.

He is.

Prayer: Lord, I want to still my heart as I kneel before you, waiting upon your guidance. Amen.

Accept it all; reject it all.

*All Scripture is God-breathed and is useful for teaching, rebuking, correcting and training <u>in righteousness</u>, so that the man of God may be thoroughly equipped for every good work.* (2Timothy 3:16 – 17)

Here's a reminder: there is no fence to sit on when it comes to salvation. You're in the kingdom, or you're out. Another important point of decision is to recognize the sovereignty of God's word. His Word is holy just as God is holy.

You either accept his word or reject it in its entirety. You don't get to "cherry-pick" the parts you like and leave the parts you think are unreasonable or contrary to your beliefs or agenda. I have heard so many times that it's too hard to live up to what the Bible requires. Yes, it's hard. I don't recall hearing the Lord say it was going to be easy. In fact, he says several times that it will require everything we have to live as he has commanded us.

Think about the Israelites of the Old Testament. How many times did they whine about how hard life was for them? How many times did they ignore the warnings God sent to them? I have been reading Jeremiah, and (in hindsight, of course) I am astounded that his people can't get the message. They are so tied up in their own ideas of who God is and how he will treat them. Sound familiar?

We constantly second guess what his Word says. Well, I think he means… Or, you can't trust what The Bible says; it's been tampered with so much, who knows what he really wanted us to do. I would challenge you to read the New Testament again, and this time, read it as a detective trying to find something that isn't consistent with God's holiness. He is a holy, sovereign God who isn't trying to trick us or change the rules in the middle of the game. He still wants what is best for us, and what is best for us is to accept his word as intended – a blueprint for capturing the abundant life he promised.

When we try to parse scripture out into what we think we can swallow, we discredit the entire thing. We should try to live boldly in his Word. Take on the tough challenges: obedience, surrender, witness, and truth; all of it, all the time.

He promises we won't be disappointed.

And, I believe him.

Prayer: Lord, help me live the abundant life you promised by trusting in your Word completely. Amen.

Growing Up to Be Somebody Nobody Likes

*Children, obey your parents as the Lord wants, because this is the right thing to do. The command says, "honor our father and mother." This is the first command that has a promise with it – "Then everything will be well with you, and you will have a long life on earth." Fathers, do not make your children angry, but raise them with the training and teaching of the Lord.* (Ephesians 6:1 – 4)

Our son Evan was notorious for getting himself into trouble. He just didn't know when to quit – or he couldn't stop himself. We've debated that topic more than once. Anyone who knew Evan knew he could be a challenge. I remember reading Ephesians 6:4 (*Do not provoke your child to anger…*) and picturing his angry little face when he was being disciplined. And then his not-so-little teenage face, still defiant, still angry.

I learned that provoking a child to anger relates more to being unfair, or irrational with punishment. Of course, when you're growing up, all punishment seems unfair. The real lesson is in discerning punishment from abuse. I always said anyone who didn't understand (not condone) child abuse never had a child who wouldn't do what you said – ever. Every word was an opportunity to rebel.

The difference lies in the motivation. Are you taking your anger about your own life circumstances out on your child? Or, are you disciplining that child because he has broken the rules through defiant acts? Dr. James Dobson reminds us to "tame the will without breaking the spirit." Now there's a challenge. I confess we walked a fine line sometimes, not sure if we were taming his will or just keeping him in line.

Sometimes I kept going just because I am as stubborn as he is. I learned to discern childish irresponsibility from open defiance. All kids forget the rules, lose their gloves, can't find their backpacks two minutes before the bus comes. Some kids, however, openly disobey. When you draw the line in the sand and say don't cross it, they are the ones who can't help but put a toe over, look you in the eye and dare you to do something about it. Take the challenge!

As a parent it is so difficult to carry out the threats we make. How many times have you said "if you do that again…"? It requires getting up, leaving the TV or video game, turning off your phone, not to mention actually carrying out the punishment. I never liked doing it, never liked the tears – mine as well as his.

But what happens if we don't discipline our children? What happens if we give in to them every time the situation gets a little ugly? I've watched that happen over the years as well. The result is that child grows up to be self-absorbed, unwilling to share things and feelings, pushes blame on to everyone around him, refusing to take responsibility. As a result, he grows up to be somebody nobody likes.

Is that what you want for your child???? We would do well to follow the Lord's leading when it comes to discipline. Read Hebrews 12: 1- 12. The Lord disciplines us for good. He wants us to learn how to be disciplined so we can share in His Holiness – so we can experience his peace. Now that's something I want for my children and grandchildren!

For some of us, this time of disciplining our children has passed. We hope we did a good job despite the mistakes we made along the way. The most we can do today is ask God to continue his discipline of their hearts so they are willing to serve him and be strong parents themselves. It won't be easy for them. Consistent discipline takes time, effort and endurance.

But, take heart, being consistent, disciplining with love and being as fair as possible, paid off. Evan has brought us so much more joy than any frustrations we experienced when he was growing up.

And, guess what? He grew up to be somebody everybody likes.

Prayer: Discipline me, Lord, and make me like you in all ways. Amen.

Is That All There Is?

*If only for **this** life we have hope in Christ, we are of all people most to be pitied.* (1 Corinthians 15:19)

Way back in 1969, Peggy Lee had a hit song called "Is That All There Is"? It was a very depressing tune outlining all the things that had happened in her life that should have been exhilarating but left her feeling empty and wishing for more. Its message was: If that's all there is, let's keep dancing; this earth is all there is so let's have a good time while we're here. We're going to die and still be asking the question, is that all there is?

What a downer. Yet, it reached #11 on the pop charts that year. Our country was in the midst of the Vietnam War, protests in the streets, the draft lottery looming in November. So, a song about depression, hopelessness and giving in to it would be a hit. We've been through many of these times in our history – the history of the world in fact. And the reason is -- we are living on earth, ruled by the evil and selfish nature of man. The good news is that God has a plan to restore us to a new heaven and a new earth where his love and power will reign. We won't be singing songs of sadness but of joy!

Here are a few of God's promises through his Word – which we can rely on for truth and hope:

"We have this hope (that God fulfills his promises) as an anchor for the soul, firm and secure." (Hebrews 6:19a)

"Heaven and earth will pass away, but my words will never pass away. (Matthew 24:35)

Then I saw "a new heaven and a new earth,"[a] for the first heaven and the first earth had passed away, and there was no longer any sea. [2] I saw the Holy City, the new Jerusalem, coming down out of heaven from God, prepared as a bride beautifully dressed for her husband. ³ And I heard a loud voice from the throne saying, "Look! God's dwelling place is now among the people, and he will dwell with them. They will be his people, and God himself will be with them and be their God.⁴ 'He will wipe every tear from their eyes. There will be no more death'[b] or mourning or crying or pain, for the old order of things has passed away." ⁵ He who was seated on the throne said, 'I am making everything new!' Then he said, 'Write this down, for these words are trustworthy and true.'" (Revelation 21:1-5)

There is a new day coming when we will all be forced to declare our love and loyalty to Jesus forever – or disown him.

He is all there is.

Prayer: I am thine, O, Lord. All my hope is in You. Amen.

A Good Deal

*What is more, I consider everything a loss compared to the surpassing greatness of knowing Christ Jesus my Lord, for whose sake I have lost all things. I consider them rubbish, that I may gain Christ.* (Philippians 3: 8)

I am an inveterate shopper. I don't always buy, but I love to look at the array of merchandise available today. But more than shopping, I love a good bargain! I once got a pair of Stuart Weitzman shoes for $65; for those of you who couldn't care less, the original price was $285. Even better, I got a Coach purse for $50! I just happened to be browsing the clearance table, and there it was. I picked it up just as another woman spied it, and she followed me around for ten minutes waiting for me to put it down. Not a chance. And I know a good deal when I see one. I can spot a bargain at a 100 paces. Just kidding – maybe.

The best deal I ever got was trading my sorrow and pain for the peace and joy of knowing Jesus. He took my sin and selfishness to the Cross so that I could know the grace and love he offers in return. Paul tells the church in Philippi that he considers everything he has gained a total loss in comparison to what he now knows in Jesus. That's quite a statement.

While the Lord may not require it of me, I am willing to give up my possessions. He has blessed me more than I could ever imagine. To stay anchored in the reality of "it's all just temporary," I often challenge myself to mentally name the five things (non-essentials) I would take with me if I ever had to give up my home and possessions. I know it probably will never happen, but it forces me to sort out my physical priorities and keep the value of "things" in the right perspective. Try it sometime; you'll be amazed at what you could truly live without when you stop to think about it.

Remember, you came into the world with nothing, and you will leave with nothing. It's where you're going that's important. Trade your sorrow for joy, your fears for peace, your sin for grace, your own world for eternity.

You'll get the best end of the bargain.

Prayer: Dear Jesus, I am so thankful for your paying for my sins. Help me keep my eyes on you. Amen.

## I Wish I Had vs I'm Glad I Did

*Behold, I am coming soon! My reward is with me, and I will give to every one according to what he has done.* (Revelation 22:12)

I remember reading a poem by John Greenleaf Whittier when I was in high school, and the phrase that has stayed with me all these years is: "Of all sad words of tongue or pen, the saddest are these: It might have been."

In the scripture verse, Jesus is talking to John as part of His revelation at the close of God's Holy Word. He is reminding us that we have limited time to accomplish God's work here on earth. Either we will be taken to heaven by death or by the great "sweeping up" into the clouds on the day of Christ's return. Each of us will stand before Jesus, he will recount our accomplishments, and we will receive our reward accordingly. We will also hear our transgressions – every harsh word, every missed opportunity, every gossipy conversation, etc. I'm not looking forward to that part. I am grateful that Jesus will be there to wipe these sins away.

The key here is to realize that when we profess Jesus as our Savior, there are expectations that we will do his work. We don't get to heaven by good works; we get there by our belief that Christ died for each of us and was raised from the dead. It is more that we are <u>compelled</u> to live for him, work for him, suffer for him, and share his love every day. He doesn't need an army of workers; he could do the work himself with a wave of his hand. But, he delights in our willingness to serve him and our fellow man as the outright declaration of our salvation.

We make excuses for what we wish we had done and didn't do. I was afraid, I wasn't sure it would be the right thing. I didn't have time. I thought someone else would do it. I like to keep my spiritual side to myself. Well, I challenge each of you to think carefully about what might have been if you had reached out, held up, fed, supported, cried with, prayed for, smiled at… someone who really needed the love of Jesus.

We hear all about the bad in our world. Remember <u>we</u> represent the good. We are Jesus' hands and feet; we do the unexpected. I want so much to tell the "other side" that if we would all just do what Jesus told us to do (Love the Lord your God with all your heart, soul, mind and strength. And love your neighbor as yourself.), we would live in a wonderful world – just as God intended.

Don't stand before the Lord on your judgment day crying with regret for what might have been. Stand before him saying, I'm glad I did!

He'll take care of the rest.

Prayer: I stand before you today, Lord, ready and willing to serve you and my neighbor. Amen.

Reverse the Curse.

*The Lord is slow to anger and abounding in steadfast love, forgiving iniquity and transgression, but he will by no means clear the guilty, visiting the iniquity of the fathers on the children, to the third and the fourth generation.* (Numbers 14:18)

*There is therefore now no condemnation for those who are in Christ Jesus. For the law of the Spirit of life has set you free in Christ Jesus from the law of sin and death. (*Romans 8:1, 2)

I heard this phrase, reverse the curse, as I was driving home the other day. It was in the context of an open discussion on ending the curse of addiction through several generations of a family. The caller was a young man who wanted to stop the cycle of alcoholism that had passed from his grandfather to his father and was now threatening him as well. I thought it was a good description of what he wanted to accomplish in his new life with Christ.

There are so many addictions to choose from these days, but we shouldn't be surprised by the number of them. Read Ecclesiastes. This book of the Bible has been attributed to King Solomon who was king of Israel during an especially prosperous and peaceful time. He was the wisest, richest, most benevolent king, even to the point of being sought after by gentiles who wanted to gain from his wisdom and business sense.

Unfortunately, King Solomon decided to test the limits of pleasure in every sense. He indulged himself in every debauchery he could find – and he didn't need a computer or the internet to help him along.

Read Ecclesiastes 2: 10 – 11. What was his conclusion? There is nothing new under the sun. We just think we have come up with something new to tempt our senses, bring us pleasure, or soothe our emotional pain. Not so.

And Solomon's road to hell was just the beginning of the same journey for his son who continued into self-satisfaction and ruin. He ruled over the land of Israel when it split and became Israel and Judah. Because of his self-indulgence, ten of the twelve tribes of Israel rebelled and formed their own kingdom.

What a disaster! God's kingdom was shattered, and God allowed its natural consequences to play out. Father and son had destroyed what was beautiful and good.

Sound familiar? The difference today is that if we call on the name of Jesus, we can change the direction of our journey. We don't have to follow in the destructive footsteps of our fathers, mothers, or grandparents. We only have to drop to our knees and ask for his help.

No matter how much pain has trickled down through the generations, we are no longer bound by it as our ancestors in the Old Testament. We won't be punished by God for the sins of our fathers. Take heart. There is nothing new under the sun, nothing God cannot overcome. If you are struggling with an addiction, make today the first day of your new life in Christ.

You can reverse the curse.

Prayer: Lord, whatever my sin, whatever my curse, I give it to you and want to change my life. Amen.

Broken Beauty

*He heals the brokenhearted and binds up their wounds.* (Psalm 147:3)

When our church moved to our new location, we took only two of the stained glass windows: Jesus in the garden of Gethsemane and one with sun rays with the final words of John Wesley. They are beautiful and meaningful to those of us who have belonged to our church for a long time. But it got me to thinking about how those windows were made. They both started as broken pieces of glass.

Do you ever feel as if you are broken into pieces? I certainly do. Life is hard. I can't really remember a time when I could say it was truly easy. I didn't say I'm not happy, but happiness isn't meant to be easily won. We have to work at it, finding it in places we might miss if we don't stay tuned into what the Lord has in store for us.

Think about the passage in Matthew 11: "Come to me, all you who are weary and burdened, and I will give you rest. Take my yoke upon you and learn from me, for I am gentle and humble in heart, and you will find rest for your souls. For my yoke is easy, and my burden is light." (Vs 28 – 30)

Come to me – crawl up into the arms of Jesus and rest there. He is waiting to give you comfort.

Take my yoke upon you and learn from me – adopt the ways of the Lord, learn his Word, keep his commandments.

For I am gentle and humble in heart – what more could we ask of the perfect role model?

You will find rest for your souls – doesn't that sound wonderful? Rest, complete and total respite from the burdens we load on our backs, given freely and lovingly to anyone who seeks it. And not just a moment of rest, but eternal rest for our souls.

For my yoke is easy and my burden is light – there is nothing difficult about giving the load we carry to Jesus and taking his yoke upon our shoulders instead. He offers us unending forgiveness and grace if we turn our burden over to him.

Can't you just feel yourself getting lighter???? Like tiny pieces of glass being built into something strong, solid, beautiful. He heals all wounds, carries all burdens, replaces our broken lives with something new and beautiful.

The artist of the picture of Jesus praying in the garden of Gethsemane is Heinrich Hofman. It is one of the most copied works of art in the world. If you look closely at Jesus' face, you can see the conflicting emotions of fear, longing, and determination. According to scripture, it is here that Jesus says to his Father, "if it is not possible for this cup to be taken away unless I drink it, may your will be done." (Matthew 26:39)

And so he goes willingly to the Cross. For you, for me, for every sinner born and yet to be born – a sacrifice so beautiful it outshines even the most celebrated of stained glass windows.

What are the broken pieces in your life? Give them to Jesus and watch as he forms them into something beautiful.

Prayer: Jesus, I give you the broken pieces of my life and ask you to make something beautiful. Amen.

Good Ole #10

*For I received from the Lord that which I also delivered to you, that the Lord Jesus in the night in which He was betrayed took bread; and when He had given thanks, He broke it and said, "This is My body, which is for you; do this in remembrance of Me." In the same way He took the cup also after supper, saying, "This cup is the new covenant in My blood; do this, as often as you drink it, in remembrance of Me." For as often as you eat this bread and drink the cup, you proclaim the Lord's death until He comes. (*1 Corinthians 11:23-26)

My niece sent me a Ron Santo commemorative patch to honor the passing of the Cub's great third baseman. I am getting ready to sew it on the sleeve of my Cubs jersey so I can wear the #10 patch proudly at Spring training in March. We sports nuts go to great lengths to preserve the memory of our beloved players.

Too bad we don't always do the same for Jesus.

He left us a commemorative sacrament, and we tend to go through the motions when taking communion. We chew the bread, drink the juice, say the responses on auto pilot. The verses in 1 Corinthians serve as a reminder that this act of eating and drinking symbolizes for us the new covenant Jesus made with all of us on the night he was betrayed. He is telling us to remember him, commemorate this act of sacrifice, honor his memory and this new life he is offering through his blood.

The next time you take communion listen carefully to the words being said. Listen with your whole heart. Rejoice in the revelation of this new covenant that wipes out sin and death forever for those who believe in a risen Savior. It is the reason we have hope.

Confess your sins, eat, drink and be cleansed.

Prayer: Lord, I confess to you I have been on auto-pilot when taking communion. Wake me up! Amen.

## What Does It Mean for God to Be For Us?

*If God is for us, who can be against us? He who did not spare his own Son, but gave him up for us all—how will He not also, along with him, graciously give us all things?* (Romans 8: 31b – 32)

We're a little sports crazy at our house. I vow each spring not to get so involved in the baseball season that I wind my life around when the Cubs are playing on TV. Don't laugh; we're still hoping for that golden season. This is the year!

I like to think God is cheering for me as well. He is for me in that he wants the best for me. And the best was his very own Son. How could I not be completely, unconditionally thankful? How could I not go through each day full of hope and joy? Truly, if God is in my corner, what could possibly get in my way?

Well, let me see – how about my own stubbornness, willful desires, bad moods, selfishness, unquestioning acceptance of the world around me? Can you relate? Take a few moments to meditate on the verse from Romans. Think about what those words really mean – He is the constant in my life. He is the only one I need. He will provide everything and everyone necessary for me to live for him. Nothing and no one can stop him from loving me. Isn't that amazing???

If you can't think of any specifics regarding what could get in the way, read Romans 8: 35 – 39. Again his promise is clearly stated – "nothing can separate us from the love of God that is in Christ Jesus our Lord." NOTHING.

- He loves us.
- He intercedes for us with his Father.
- He protects us – many times from ourselves.
- He calls to us over the noise in our lives.

- He comforts us.
- He brings us joy.
- He provides each new day and the opportunity to serve him.

The list is endless. Buy a notebook and begin your list. Add to it each time you receive something that reminds you of his love. You will never run out of new ways to praise him. And when you are having a bad day, take out your notebook and just read out loud.

Once again, you will know that nothing can separate you from the God who loved you so much that he gave his only Son for you.

Prayer: Thank you, Jesus, for never leaving me. Praise be to God. Amen.

Could Be Better, Could Be Worse…

*This is the day the Lord has made; let us be glad and rejoice in it.* (Psalm 118:24)

My birthday was last week, and as many of us who are getting older do, we joked about how having another birthday beats the alternative. My dad used to say that any day above ground is a good day. Our friend Bill used to say, "Could be better, could be worse; could be ridin' in a hearse." He called it nursing home humor. I like their attitude.

We need to live in the day. God made it for us to enjoy for his glory.

When we look too far ahead or live in the past, we defeat God's purpose for us. My daughter and I used to discuss it all the time. She had a tendency to project too far ahead and imagine all kinds of things that could go wrong. Most of them didn't. She learned to rein in her galloping toward imagined disaster. Now that she has five kids, she only has time to thank the Lord for getting through one day. And that's a good thing. Life has a way of teaching us what really matters.

My husband's aunt, on the other hand, lived in the past. She continually talked about all of the painful things that had happened to her family. It was a downer. She wasn't angry or self-pitying; she just talked way too much about things that happened years ago and how life would have been different if she could have changed things (things, by the way, that were out of her control).

Neither approach to life brings us any closer to living in the day as consistent, faithful, willing followers of Christ. Don't misunderstand; you need to learn from the past and plan for the future. But, dwelling too long in either place robs you of the joy of today. Don't borrow trouble, and don't linger on past trouble either. It's just that – past. Turn your energies to the business of today and thank Jesus that he has given you this day to honor him.

Stop right now and say thanks. Read all of Psalm 118. The Lord is good and his love endures forever.

Prayer: Lord, keep me in the moment. Amen.

## The Price of Everything; the Value of Nothing

*Do not store up for yourselves treasures on earth, where moth and rust destroy, and where thieves break in and steal. But store up for yourselves treasures in heaven, where moth and rust do not destroy, and where thieves do not break in and steal. For where your treasure is, there your heart will be also.* (Matthew 6:19 – 21)

I was breezing through some catalogs the other night; it's my entertainment sometimes, like window shopping. Across the pages I noted a big difference in prices. It struck me that I knew way too much about what these items (clothes, shoes, handbags, household things) should cost. I can tell you if the cloth is worth the money, and if a designer handbag is real or fake. Seriously, does anyone really need to know that?

It reminded me of conversations with a friend who can tell me the exact dollar amount he spent on each item in their home, their cars, their clothes, restaurants, even charitable donations. Everything is expensive and top quality, and they are, of course, the most generous of everyone they know. However, when we get to other topics such as Jesus, eternity, and salvation, he has a harder time placing value. These things seem to have no value, in fact. He and his wife are defined by what they own, what they spend, and what they do for others. Kind of takes the shine off the glowing deed, doesn't it?

We are all guilty of bragging about what we have or what we have done. It's part of the human condition. We very often judge things and people through worldly eyes. What price does the world place on this item or that job? What will the neighbors think of our new car? Our new house? Our new (fill in the blank)? Do we ever ask the Lord what he thinks of those same treasures?

I'll give you a hint: read the scripture above. When we store up treasures here on earth to define ourselves as important, when we place ultimate value on things rather than people and relationships, when we forget who made us and bask in the glow of earthly success, we lose our sense of reality that is grounded in heavenly purpose. We long for recognition; we pursue human praise, all the while forgetting that real praise, real recognition is given by our Lord and Savior Jesus Christ. His attention to the details of our lives never waivers or depends upon our worldly works. All we have to do to gain his recognition is "confess with our lips that Jesus is Lord and believe in our hearts that God raised him from the dead…" (Romans 10:9).

Where are your treasures? Take an inventory of what is truly important to you, what you couldn't give up. Then ask the Lord to rate them for you. I'm guessing his top ten list is different than mine. He's big on feelings, truths, loving your neighbor as yourself, laying down your life for your friend. I'm a little more into bragging about my grandchildren, adoring each one of them, buying them things they don't need and lavishing my undivided attention on them.

Idols, you say? Yes. But I'm working on it. I want very much to put Jesus first. I want to lavish my praise on him and follow his Word. It's one of my constant prayers.

What can I say? I'm a work in progress.

Prayer: Lord, I want to put you first in everything. Praise the Lord! Amen.

Choose to Be Joyful.

*May the God of hope fill you with **all joy** and peace as you trust in him, so that you may overflow with hope by the power of the Holy Spirit.* (Romans 15:13)

If you track the word *joy* through the New Testament, you will find it is often paired with words like hope, peace, and complete. I think it is emphasizing the fact that joy is a state of mind, not just a feeling.

We can choose to be joyful. Circumstances can rob us of our happy feelings, but the joy of the Lord is complete and cannot be lost. It is given to us through our knowledge of the Holy Spirit which we receive when we commit our hearts to Jesus. What a wonderful promise! That deep joy we know is there even when we are grieving, unhappy, or despairing.

I lost my brother John to cancer in 2009. The grief has been overwhelming at times, but he would be happy to know that I have not resigned my joy to my pain. My joy in knowing I have eternal life in Christ is the over-riding truth. John taught me to trust in the Lord no matter what, even when we lose someone we love so much. Psalm 30:5b tells us "Weeping may last through the night, but joy comes with the morning."

It is the deep inner joy that outlasts our sorrow; the promise of a continuing and constant relationship with the Savior. Sometimes we have to work at it, but that joy is there and will come to the surface when we call on it.

I have always told our kids they can choose to be happy. But, I like this choice even better. My hope for them was to create a mindset that turned to the positive more often than the negative – a conscious choice to be happy. And, even though we may be wired to be more one way than the other, we can still choose.

And, when we accept Christ into our hearts as our Savior, we make the choice to live with an ever-strengthening, deep down, heartfelt joy.

Prayer: Lord, I am thankful for a joyful heart. Amen.

## Treasures

*When they had seen him, they spread the word concerning what had been told them about this child, and all who heard it were amazed at what the shepherds said to them. But Mary treasured up all these things and pondered them in her heart.* (Luke 2:17 – 19)

It's what mothers do, hold onto little pieces of memories they can treasure. When our daughter was in high school, I presented a program to the faculty during an in-service training day. I just happened to see Erica in the library when I came to give the program. I told her I was a little nervous, and she said "it's so great you're doing this; now they'll all know how wonderful you are, too." It was the "too" that got me – she thinks I'm wonderful! What a treasure in my heart!

I could list so many of these treasures from both my children and grandchildren, but the message is a universal one for mothers: be there to collect your treasures. One of the girls I used to work with had two small children and worked full time. She was expressing her frustration that her two year old son still wanted to be rocked at night – something she didn't have time for right now. I told her to rock that little guy for as long as she could. The time would come sooner than she realized when he didn't need to be held in her arms before he went to sleep. I encouraged her to hold him each night and truly enjoy the time.

We went on to other jobs, and when I ran into her a few years later, she told me how she had taken my advice. She had enjoyed another year of rocking time – and treasured those minutes now that her son was becoming so independent. "I'm so glad I didn't miss out," she said.

We all face similar times of being pulled in many directions. It seems the job of building strong children is more than we can handle with all of the other pressures of our world. But the rewards are well worth the effort.

The Lord's mother carried a heavy load – raising the Savior of the world! But, you know, she relied on the same God we do. He is just as much there for us – mother *and* father – as he was for Mary and His Son. What an awesome God!

What treasures have you collected? Write them down and give God the credit. Also, think about the times you have relied on him to give you the guidance you needed regarding your children – and the times you should have. We are so quick to react and handle challenges our own way. Why not turn them over to the Lord and wait for his response? He promises "if any of you lacks wisdom, you should ask God, who gives generously to all without finding fault, and it will be given to him." (James 1:5)

He loves to be in the details! Open your life to him today.

Prayer: Lord, I give you my treasures and my heart. Amen.

Heaven On a Spoon

*On this mountain the* LORD *Almighty will prepare*

*a feast of rich food for all peoples,*

*a banquet of aged wine—*

*the best of meats and the finest of wines.*

*On this mountain he will destroy*

*the shroud that enfolds all peoples,*

*the sheet that covers all nations;*

*he will swallow up death forever.*

*The Sovereign* LORD *will wipe away the tears*

*from all faces;*

*he will remove his people's disgrace*

*from all the earth.*

*The* LORD *has spoken.* (Isaiah 25: 6-8)

One of my guilty pleasures is treating myself to a turtle sundae. The combination of salty and sweet is a little bit of heaven on a spoon. The first time I ordered one I said Bob and I could share, but that didn't work out too well for him.

I like to think that little bit of heaven is just a foretaste of the glory I will enjoy when my time comes to join Jesus. The prophet, Isaiah, clearly outlined the promise of an eternal life: "He will swallow up death forever." We can anticipate a fabulous feast, one that will never end! Just think, the equivalent of a turtle sundae all day, every day! His love never ends; his caring never ends.

As we celebrate our holiday joy with cookies, candy canes and the annual food fest, think about how these goodies are just a prelude to the glorious feast we will enjoy in the presence of our Savior, Jesus Christ who was born in Bethlehem and died on Golgotha. He came to conquer death and offer a beautiful eternity to each of us.

"Taste and see that the Lord is good." (Psalm 34:8)

Prayer: Remind me, Lord, how good you are and that you have saved us from eternal death. Amen.

Getting What We Deserve... or Not

*I will punish you as your deeds deserve, declares the Lord.* (Jeremiah 21:14)

*Are you, perhaps, misinterpreting God's generosity and patient mercy towards you as weakness on his part? Don't you realize that God's kindness is meant to lead you to repentance?* Romans 2:4 (Paraphrased)

*Like the rest, we were by nature objects of wrath. But because of his great love for us, God, who is rich in mercy, made us alive with Christ even when we were dead in transgressions--it is by grace you have been saved.* (Ephesians 2:3-5)

In the book of Job, God allows Satan to bring calamity to Job in order to prove Job's true love for God. Satan maintains that Job only loves God and keeps his commandments because Job is rich and has been blessed by God. Satan declares that if all of Job's wealth, family, and possessions are taken away, he will curse God. The conventional wisdom of the day was that sin and punishment go hand in hand and, therefore, Job must have sinned greatly in order to bring such devastation on himself.

But Job holds fast to the facts: he has neither sinned nor turned from God. He maintains his righteousness and cannot understand why these tragedies are happening to him. He cries out to God, "I don't deserve this; I am righteous before you."

How many times have we come to the Lord full of indignation? I'm a good person; I help others; I love the Lord. I DON'T deserve this pain.

But, think about this: do you deserve God's mercy? Do you deserve his forgiveness? Did Jesus die for you because you deserved salvation?

Not in the least. If we want to get into a match with God about what we deserve, we need to be careful.

We don't live under the same conditions that Job did. He maybe had a right to cling to his righteousness and demand an explanation from God. He had kept the Law. (He also got caught up in his own power to live a righteous life, and God reminds him of his insignificance.)

But we live under Grace, the free gift of God through Jesus Christ. The whole dynamic changes. We no longer grasp at the details of the Law. We no longer keep a tally of everything we have done right and wrong -- and neither does God.

So the next time you are deep in that pity party, crying that you don't deserve what you are getting, remember the Cross of Jesus and rejoice that you aren't getting what you **really** deserve – eternal death.

Prayer: Lord, thank you for sparing me the pain of getting what I really deserve. Amen.

Christmas Crack

*Woe to those who call evil good and good evil, who put darkness for light and light for darkness, who put bitter for sweet and sweet for bitter!* (Isaiah 5:20)

I have discovered the most wonderful indulgence; it's called "Christmas Crack" and is almost as good as heaven on a spoon. No, it isn't really a drug, but it could be. One handful of this sweet concoction, and you will be hooked! It is also called "reindeer chow" in case you want to be more politically correct. Either way, it is good (taste) covering bad (calories)!

It is easy, however, to be fooled when it comes to good and evil. Beware of those things or people in your life who offer what seems to be good, but in the end, turns into something bad. I'm talking about being deceived into thinking that this life is all there is, about accepting the darkness, about living in unhappiness because you think there isn't anything else.

There is more. There is light. There is good. We may not always see it because of the evil in this world, but there is a wonderful little space in each of us where good resides. It is often covered with the blackness of sin, an untreated mental illness, a stubborn heart, a hurt so deep you cannot believe it can be healed, but the good is still there and will answer to the call of Jesus when you accept his love and forgiveness.

Give some thought to how Jesus came into this world to be its light. John 1: 4 – 5 says, "In him was life, and that life was the light of all mankind. The light shines in the darkness, and the darkness has not overcome it." His light shines for us so we can distinguish between good and evil, what is right or wrong, what is uplifting or degrading.

He is NEVER going to lead you astray. He will not ask you to accept only the bitter; he will guide you to the sweet – whatever it is.

So, while you are enjoying some "Christmas Crack," remember why we celebrate. Jesus came to live among us and to be a sacrifice for our sins. He brings each of us an eternal life.

How sweet it is!

Prayer: Lord, thank you for always leading me down the true course you have set for me. Amen.

Preparing the Way

*Then Jesus was led up by the Spirit into the wilderness to be tempted by the devil.* (Matthew 4: 1 – 1)

Ash Wednesday is the day that marks the beginning of the Lenten season for Christians. Traditionally, members of the faith celebrate this season to commemorate Jesus' wilderness experience when he fasted and prayed and was harassed by the devil. Today, we acknowledge the beginning of this period of prayer and fasting by wearing a mark of ashes on our foreheads. These ashes are usually the remains of the burning of palm branches from the Palm Sunday service the prior year. They are a reminder of Christ's suffering.

At one Ash Wednesday service I attended, the minister asked each person to write a problem, challenge, or temptation on a piece of paper. We then placed the papers in a metal container, and he set them on fire. As the ashes cooled, we prayed for each other and the "sufferings" that had now become ashes. We then received the ash cross on our foreheads and vowed to accept that these problems had been given to Jesus, and he would do with them as he decided was best for us. It was a beautiful moment. It still reminds me of the vast power of giving our problems to the Lord, no matter what day it is.

Some Christians practice self-denial during this Lenten period; they give up something precious to them in order to suffer in some small measure for God. Others focus more on the culmination of this period – Easter – when we celebrate Christ's resurrection. It doesn't matter really how you acknowledge the importance of Lent, just that you know its purpose. Not only did Christ suffer on the Cross, he suffered much during his time here on earth – and he endured it for us.

Hebrews 4: 15 tells us the reason: "For we do not have a high priest who is unable to sympathize with our weaknesses, but we have one who has been tempted in every way, just as we are--yet was without sin."

He knows about sin; he knows about us. He knows even before we confess to him that we have sinned. And yet, he loves us with a love so deep that we can't even comprehend it.

Hallelujah!

Prayer: Thank you, Jesus for suffering for me. I never want to forget your sacrifice. Amen.

Re-evaluating

*Give, and it will be given to you. A good measure, pressed down, shaken together and running over, will be poured into your lap. For with the measure you use, it will be measured to you.* (Luke 6:38)

There are a lot of things that sound good. We are bombarded with promises every day in the hundreds of 30 – 60 second sound bites telling us we can be beautiful, rich, successful, and happy. Not all of them produce the returns they promise.

One promise you can count on, though, is the one in Luke 6: *Give and it will be given to you.* Sounds a little like the Golden Rule – with a twist. This one promises abundance, not just an equal return of good for good: "A good measure, pressed down, shaken together and <u>running over</u>, will be poured into your lap." How great is that! And all I have to do is give? Easy peasy as my grandkids say. And, you know what – it is that easy.

This passage comes from the Sermon on the Plains which is Luke's reinforcement of parts of the Sermon on the Mount found in Matthew 5 - 7. Jesus is reminding his people to live according to the principles he has laid out for them: be humble; be generous with each other; love your enemies; be merciful. He knew life was going to get really hard really fast, and he wanted them to be able to hold each other up under the strain. Those words are just as appealing today as they were then. Think about being humble, merciful, generous, and loving – what is the result? I know what you're thinking. What if the other person isn't the same towards me? The answer is this: Jesus sees what you do and will increase it to the point of running over.

It's not a zero-sum game here. We're talking about what you do because you love Jesus – that's the focus, not just getting back from anyone you're generous toward. The abundance, the joy, the satisfaction comes in giving out of a love for Jesus who loved you so much he was willing to die for you.

So, here's a new 3 step plan:

1. Live abundantly!
2. Share abundantly!
3. Repeat Steps 1 and 2!

The returns are immeasurable.

Prayer: Lord, help me to live the abundant life you have provided for me. Amen.

Grains of Sand

*How precious to me are your thoughts, O God! How vast is the sum of them, Were I to count them, they would outnumber the grains of sand. When I am awake, I am still with you.* (Psalm 139:17-18)

While resting on the beach, I started thinking about this Bible verse and its significance to my understanding of how much God loves me. I looked up and down the stretch of beach that fronted our hotel and thought how massive a task it would be to count the grains of sand on just that one hundred feet. It is mind boggling to think that God has more thoughts of each of us than ALL the grains of sand!

How does he do that???? He is God. He can do anything. He knows everything. I would be impressed if the verse said his thoughts would outnumber the grains of sand in an hourglass. But it is talking about all of the grains of sand that exist.

If God is engaged in our lives to this extent, we should be forever grateful! When you think about the number of thoughts you have in a day, remember God's thoughts are exponentially, even infinitely, more numerous. And his thoughts are compassionate, empathetic, sacred thoughts – about YOU. Can you say the same about your own thoughts? I certainly can't. Most of my thoughts are infinitely selfish.

The next time you see any sand, a beach, even a sandbox, think about the thoughts God has for you. Think about the concern, care and love he has for you.

Rejoice in that knowledge.

Prayer: Lord, I rejoice in the knowledge that your thoughts of me are too numerous to count. Amen.

Time

*But the day of the Lord will come like a thief, and then the heavens will pass away with a roar, and the heavenly bodies will be burned up and dissolved, and the earth and the works that are done on it will be exposed. Since all these things are thus to be dissolved, what sort of people ought you to be in lives of holiness and godliness, waiting for and hastening the coming of the day of God,...* (2Peter 3: 10 – 14)

Many of us have the feeling that we have all the time in the world to accomplish what we want. But, as the scripture reminds us, time is going to run out. There will come a day when Jesus will call us home, and those who know him as Savior will be caught up in the clouds.

I especially like the verse, "and the heavenly bodies will be burned up and dissolved, and the earth and the works that are done on it will be exposed." What earthly pursuits have you been involved with that will be exposed on that final day? I have been convicted over the past few weeks about the way I spend my time. I can waste a lot of it. I can sleep it away. I can just sit.

This is unusual for me. I was always busy, busy, busy. My kids used to tease me that I had two speeds, high and off. I would literally work until I dropped into bed and would fall asleep immediately. Now that my life has slowed down in retirement, I'm not sure where I lost that drive to find projects, volunteer, accomplish something every day.

It may be because I have re-defined accomplishment. I no longer feel up to the BIG projects. I get tired more easily; I get frustrated more quickly when things get difficult. I would rather think and read than plan and do. Maybe I used up all my energy in the first 60 years of my life.

Yet, I am sure the Lord has work for me to do. I hear his call in the pain I see around me. I see his hand at work in the healing of friends and know that God needs me to pray and support those he heals. I could spend the greater part of every day praying for, listening to, calling on, writing to my friends who need to hear about the love and power of Jesus Christ – before time runs out.

I hope that when my works are exposed, there will be enough heavenly pursuits to lay at Jesus' feet, not for my glory but his.

"And whatsoever you do in word or deed, *do all* in the name of the *Lord* Jesus" (Colossians 3:17) That is the real key. Big or small, planned project or spontaneous effort – if you are doing it for the glory of the Lord, it can survive that final exposure.

Prayer: Lord, may all my works be done for your glory. Amen.

Let Your Freak Flag Fly

*For I am not ashamed of the gospel, because it is the power of God for the salvation of everyone who believes: first for the Jew, then for the Gentile.* (Romans 1:16)

When we visited our daughter and her family after Thanksgiving, we were again treated to an excellent sermon at their church. The theme of the sermon was "tell your own story." We all have one. The minister made reference to the book of Job. Now there's a story! Fortunately, mine doesn't follow the same path of personal loss and destruction that Job experienced. But the one thing we do have in common is that I will also remain loyal to my God and Savior.

I have experienced loss, ill health, and emotional upheaval. I know you have, too. The key is to see those events in the context of an unshakable faith, a longing to serve God better and deeper in the process of healing, a promise to use those experiences as opportunities to share the power of God in your life.

So, what keeps us from telling our story? For me, it's a fear of being rejected, of losing respect, of being a stumbling block to someone's faith rather than a foundational stone. It's not that I don't share my story; it's more that I don't take opportunities as they present themselves. I think too much. I analyze too much. I use the excuse that timing is everything.

No, it isn't.

<u>God's</u> timing is everything. If he gives you an opportunity to tell your story, do it. You don't have to convince, persuade, or cajole anyone into surrender. Just tell what happened to you.

I sometimes worry about the topics I cover in my writings. I am not out to offend anyone or upset anyone. A dear friend said, "you worry too much about that." And she is right. It made me stop and think, If I truly trust God to use these messages for his glory, I don't need to worry about the details.

He will.

So what if someone calls me a Jesus freak? It's not the worst thing I've been called. If you are being called one, it just shows you are living your life for Him. Again, not the worst thing.

Just let your freak flag fly.

Prayer: Lord God, open my eyes and my heart to those who need to hear my story. Amen.

Gettin' Ready for Glory

*O LORD, our Lord, how excellent (majestic and glorious) is Your name in all the earth! You have set Your glory on the heavens.* (Psalm 8:1)

In a way, we are all getting ready for the glory that awaits us in heaven if we believe in Jesus. So, what do we do in the meantime?

It's all about living. Once you have accepted Christ as your Savior, the dying part is taken care of. We don't live as if there is nothing to look forward to. We live as if there is the BEST to look forward to.

- Live with the joy of knowing you are His.
- Live with the peace of knowing he will never leave you nor forsake you.
- Live with the expectation that he has a plan for your life and will see it to completion in the day of Jesus Christ.
- Live with the patience of someone who knows there is a better life in Glory.
- Live with kindness in your heart for those who don't know Jesus and need to see Him in you.
- Live with the knowledge of His majesty.
- Live with His strength whether you feel it within your own power or not.
- Live with holiness that honors his sacrifice for you.

And, most of all, live as if you are getting ready for glory.

You are.

Prayer: Lord, I am ready for Glory. And I give you all the praise! Amen.

Birthdays

*I tell you the truth, no one can enter the kingdom of God unless he is born of water and the Spirit.* (John 3:5)

My family celebrates twelve birthdays in the months of July, August and September. That's a lot of birthday cake! Unfortunately, not everyone is here to celebrate. We have lost some precious loved ones in the last few years. The good news is that I am sure I will see them all again -- because they didn't just celebrate their birth days but also their second birth days. There was an exact point in each of their lives when they accepted Jesus Christ as Savior and were born of water and the Spirit.

I celebrate my birthday on August 17, but my second birthday is March 15, 1979. It is the day I cried out to Jesus and said, "If you are there; if you are real, please come into my life." And he did. My life has never been the same since that night. I have cried out to God many times since then; I have cried many times since then. I have also experienced joy beyond description as I live my life for Him. There is no problem too big, no pain too great, no sorrow too deep that Jesus cannot overcome it. I would never try to tell you it's easy, but I can tell you it's true.

If you are experiencing pain, sorrow, or joy, there is no other way to experience it than through Jesus Christ. When you think you can't sink any lower or fly any higher, trust in the Lord, and you will see that you are measuring those highs and lows according to the world's yardstick. There is no comfort like the comfort of Jesus; there is no happiness as deep and enduring as when it is sent from Jesus as part of his perfect plan for your life.

Live for Him, and you will see what I mean.

So, when is your birthday? Celebrate with all your heart! And, when is your second birthday? Don't know? Make it today. All you have to do is say: "Jesus, I know I have made mistakes and lived an imperfect life. Please forgive me and come into my life."

And He will.

Prayer: Jesus, I know I have made mistakes and lived an imperfect life. Please forgive me and come into my life. Amen.

It's All About Choice.

*Blessed is the man who remains steadfast under trial, for when he has stood the test he will receive the crown of life, which God has promised to those who love him.* (James 1:12)

My husband Bob and I have been trying to follow a diet plan. Those pounds just kept creeping up on us, and we decided it was time to do something about them. We had really good intentions. I was able to make good choices for the most part. But last week I wanted a break. I really didn't want to abandon the whole plan; it's really not that difficult to follow. And, what harm could there be in falling off the wagon for a day or two?

Unfortunately, I didn't just fall off the wagon; I jumped at full speed into a ditch of donuts! And they tasted really, really good. Throw in some potato chips, and you have a full blown diet disaster. I didn't realize how much I missed junk food. But I really wanted to lose these unwanted pounds. So, I got up, dusted the powdered sugar off my face, wiped my greasy fingers and climbed back on the good food ferry.

You can all relate, I'm sure. It's the same with living out our faith. We seem to be able to avoid temptation, follow the narrow path, and live for Jesus most of the time. But then we have a bad day; someone rejects our best attempts; we fall back into a sin we thought we had conquered. No one is immune to Satan's lingering grasp. The good news is we can climb out of that pit and get back on the right path. All we have to do is confess our sin and accept the forgiveness Jesus offers. There will be consequences of course. (Like the two pounds I gained back) But nothing is insurmountable with Jesus at your side.

That's why staying in his Word, praying, and forgiving ourselves are the secrets to a successful Christian life. Count for Jesus and celebrate your joys. And, when you fall off the wagon, jump up, chase after it and get back on!

In fact, Jesus will give you a hand up – every time.

Prayer: Jesus, help me avoid temptation and live for you. Amen.

Live Like a Pro

*And let steadfastness have its full effect, that you may be perfect and complete, lacking in nothing.* (James 1:4)

What makes someone a "pro?" You know, a professional in his/her field? Some would say, it's the money, or it's the title, or it's the level of expertise. Whatever definition you use, there is a common factor in being a pro.

Practice

If you want to be a professional anything, you have to work hard. You may have talent, education, investors, even a great personality, but if you don't perfect your craft, you aren't really a pro. Or, maybe you don't need to be labeled a pro; you just want to know you are doing the best job you can. Good for you!

We don't often think of our service to God as "going pro," but it is worth considering. Would you like to be known as a professional servant? You can be. All it takes is steadfast practice of the principles of servant-hood God lays out for us in his Word.

We must be steadfast in our love for God, our prayers, our love for each other and our work to further the Kingdom of Jesus Christ. We must practice putting our own needs and desires aside and striving for perfection in obedience to him. As Paul reminds us: "Not that I have already obtained this or am already perfect, but I press on to make it my own, because Christ Jesus has made me his own. Brothers, I do not consider that I have made it my own. But one thing I do: forgetting what lies behind and straining forward to what lies ahead, I press on toward the goal for the prize of the upward call of God in Christ Jesus. Let those of us who are mature think this way, and if in anything you think otherwise, God will reveal that also to you." (Philippians 3: 12 – 13)

Do you remember the old adage, practice makes perfect? I have also heard it as perfect practice makes perfect.

So, perfect your practice in the ways of the Lord, and he will make you perfect in the day of Jesus Christ.

Prayer: Lord, I strive to be my best for you. Amen.

## Out of Sync

*Know therefore today, and lay it to your heart, that the Lord is God in heaven above and on the earth beneath; there is no other. Therefore you shall keep his statutes and his commandments, which I command you today, that it may go well with you and with your children after you, and that you may prolong your days in the land that the Lord your God is giving you for all time.* (Deuteronomy 4: 39-40)

Have you ever watched a TV program where the sound was out of sync with the picture? The words you hear are just a little bit out of step with the lips. Not much, just a little; just enough to be annoying and hard to watch. I often think that is how God sees me when I am out of sync with his commandments. Not much, just a little; just enough to show him I don't trust him to guide my steps, to live up to his promises to me, to protect me from my enemies.

It's hard for him to watch.

Do you realize God loves you so much that he hurts when he sees you doing things that are disobedient? It's because he knows you are headed for pain. His instructions are so clear. There are no conflicting messages. "Love the Lord your God with all your heart, soul, mind and strength. And love your neighbor as yourself." (Mark 12:30)

If we would be obedient only to those two, we would save ourselves (and others) a lot of trouble and pain. We might be able to restore relationships, solve world hunger and avoid war. No one would be homeless, go without meaningful work or sink into addiction. There would be a hand up and an arm around every shoulder.

Sound impossible? Yes, it is – for us humans. But, "with God, all things are possible. I can do all things through Christ who strengthens me. I can keep his statutes and his commandments." (Philippians 4:13)

I cannot stay in harmony with God or anyone else if I am not willing to rely on the truth of his Word and the power of his love.

Match the words you say with the life you live for Christ, *that you may prolong your days...*

Get in sync.

Prayer: Lord, I want to live my life in sync with you and your Word. Amen.

## Sending the Right Message

*Then I heard the voice of the Lord saying, "Whom shall I send? And who will go for us? " And I said, "Here am I. Send me!"* (Isaiah 6:8)

Sometimes I think about how small I am in the vastness of the universe. Just a tiny speck, really. How could I possibly make a difference? But then I remember the verse in Isaiah, and I am encouraged to know that the awesome God of this universe speaks to me just as he did to Old Testament prophets.

He still relies on us to carry his message, do his work, and honor him in everything we do. Our world might have changed, but God has not. My friends and I were discussing how much our world has changed just since our parents were born in the 1920's. My father's family plowed the ground with horses hitched with a harness. Both of my parents came of age during the Great Depression. They also were alive when Hiroshima and Nagasaki were being bombed, as well as the first moon landing. They went from not even having a telephone to watching cable TV and the boom of the computer age. Change, change, change.

I remember my dad saying the one constant in his life was the fact that when he was going to church and serving the Lord, life was better. What a wonderful statement to make to your children! I'm not sure if he knew what an impression that made on me. Probably not, which is another good point: we are constantly making statements or doing things that make indelible impressions on our children and grandchildren. It's a little scary, but it is also a wonderful opportunity to let them know what is important to you. We can have such a positive influence on their lives, no matter how old they are.

What are the messages you send? How do your children see you handle difficult times? Real emotion or just stiff upper lip? Praying on your knees or gutting it out on your own two feet? Ultimately finding peace in God's will or struggling to make sense of your life?

And what about handling the good times? Do you take all the credit when things are going well? Or, do you thank the Lord for his generosity and give the glory to him?

Step up.

Trust me, if you don't, someone else will. And they may not send the message your children need to hear.

Prayer: Lord, make me aware of my words. Make them words that give you the glory. Amen.

## Smile Markers

*Delight yourself in the LORD, and he will give you the desires of your heart.* (Psalm 37:4)

I heard the term "Smile Markers" on the radio on my way to an appointment. While I didn't hear what followed, it got me to thinking about the Smile Markers in my life. I could name the usual things, the birth of my children, my grandchildren, other family related times, but I tried to think about times when I was blessed unexpectedly, when the Lord truly brought a smile to my face. So, here goes.

- I was privileged to lead a Bible Study for a few people who didn't all know Jesus as their Savior. By the end of the four weeks, my dear friend who hosted the study, accepted Christ as her Savior and has been a faithful servant ever since.
- A friend from long ago has come back into my life at just the right time, and I am sure the Lord knew I needed another prayer warrior at this point.
- Two years ago this week, I discovered through my reading, new truths about God: "We exist for God, God does not exist for us."
- I have learned in the most direct way that "all things work together for good to them that love the Lord and are called according to his purpose." (Romans 8:28) It has been my favorite verse for a very long time, and the Lord proves its truth over and over. Being able to rejoice in him while learning a hard lesson is a gift only God can give.
- The day I learned to cry out to God and not worry about how my prayer was formed. My heart was broken, and he heard my cries. (Psalm 61:1)

These are only a few examples; I could list many more blessings. But you get the idea. Even when it seems there is no joy in your life, God can make you smile through his very personal intervention.

These times may not come when you think you need them, but they will come when God knows the time is right.

What are your Smile Markers? Make a list; write them down. Read them when things get to be too much for you. And take heart; God will bless you again and again if you trust and obey.

Prayer: Lord, help me to trust and obey. Amen.

Chewed Up and Spit Out

*Like newborn babies, crave pure spiritual milk, so that by it you may grow up in your salvation, now that you have tasted that the Lord is good.* (I Peter 2:2-3)

When I worked for the County Health Department in the early 1970's, I had responsibility to educate young mothers about the need for good nutrition for their newborns. Having been raised in a traditional home with baby food readily available, I was dumbstruck when I heard the visiting nurse tell a young mom, "You can't chew your table food and then give it to your baby. It's lost all of its value by then. Your baby isn't getting the good out of the food. That is why he isn't gaining weight like he should."

What? They chewed the food and then took it out of their own mouths and fed it to their babies? But it was true. The nurse explained to me that their mothers had done it that way, their grandmothers had done it that way, and so it was normal to them.

When we let someone else chew up God's Word and feed it to us, we also are losing the value. I'm not suggesting that no one else can help you learn about God's Word, but I am saying there is no substitute for studying the Bible yourself. You have to take the time to read and digest what the Scripture is saying – to YOU. He will speak to you through those beautiful words in a way that feels personal and right. I have experienced several setbacks lately, and I have literally run to my Bible to find comfort. It is the only thing that helps me find some level of peace.

I am telling you the truth: once you have invited Jesus into your life, His Word takes on an unbelievable significance. It will guide you through the most difficult times; it will relieve your guilt; it will rearrange your priorities. You will crave it just like you do food.

Remember: "All Scripture is inspired by God and is useful to teach us what is true and to make us realize what is wrong in our lives. It corrects us when we are wrong and teaches us to do what is right. God uses it to prepare and equip his people to do every good work." (2 Timothy 3:16-17) What a proclamation! How could we not trust in the sovereignty of this wonderful book? How could we not want to read it, meditate on it, and share it with everyone we know?

"Crave pure spiritual milk..." there is nothing more pure than opening God's Word and reading it for yourself. Trust that he will speak to you. Expect that he will speak to you. And THEN, find a good commentary, Bible study and/or spiritual resource.

But, don't take my word for it. Read it for yourself.

Feed on his sovereign Word, and you will grow in wisdom and strength.

Prayer: Lord, your Word is my strength. Speak to me through its pages. Amen.

First, Last, Always

*I am the Alpha and the Omega, says the Lord God, who is, and was, and who is to come, the Almighty.* (Revelation 1:8)

I had a revelation this week. It wasn't new information for me. In fact, I've struggled with it for many years – 36 years – to be exact. From the day our son was born, I have put my children first. I have indeed worshiped them. I have been lost in them. Nothing, not even my love for the Lord, has been more important. I was a stay-at-home mom so they could have a strong start in life; I went to work to provide a college education for them; I am available to them night and day. And now there are their children to worship and lavish time and attention on.

Every time the question comes up about what idols we have in our lives, my first thought is my children. Sound familiar? It's not that I did anything wrong in giving my life to them. We all want the best for our children and grandchildren. And I know they appreciate what I have done and probably aren't even aware that I have lost my own identity in them. They surely see me as a strong, committed and loving mother. And I am.

In recent weeks we have had to deal with some conflict, news of a relocation, changes -- family stuff. But in my efforts to reconcile these events with my own life and future, I realized how much I have depended upon keeping everything the same in the picture I have painted for us. In my head I know they have to live their own lives, make their own mistakes, build their own family lives, and I respect that. It's not like I try to tell them what to do all the time. But, in my heart I know that I would like to take their pain, make their best decisions, and protect them from harm. But I can't do that for them. I can't live **for** them. I can't live for **them**.

And, so, I came to the point where I didn't know how I would change this deep need to keep them at the center of my life. Can you relate to this struggle? I want the Lord to be first in my head and my heart. I want to rely on his hand to guide my every step. I don't want to live for my children because it is a futile and unforgiving path. They grow up, they move away, they lead their own lives. It is the way God intended. (Genesis 2:24)

The same God who created us to love our children with a selfless love is the same God who demands to be first in our lives.

There is no other way to live. If I keep my eyes on Jesus and make him the center of my life, I can love my children, enjoy their independence, and watch them build strong lives for themselves. But I must stand on the edge of their family circle. I can pray for them, love them, support them and share their burdens. But I cannot live for them. It's time to really, truly, finally give them to the Lord.

I'm not saying I have flipped a switch and changed my feelings overnight. It is a process just like anything else. I have to make conscious decisions every time I feel myself slipping into my old habits. I have been repeating to myself that Jesus is first. It helps. I only wish I had come to this monumental conclusion years ago.

And it is monumental. How can I describe to you the moment it all came together in my head? I'm analytical by nature. I love the "if, then" approach to any problem. So, in those terms: If I put Jesus first in my life (for real), then I can live for the One who will never leave me, move on, or even unintentionally hurt me. It's the only way.

I don't want you to think I haven't loved the Lord all this tim I know that when I committed my life to Jesus I did it sincerity. He knows that, too. He also knows of my str been patiently waiting for me to come to this instinct to give ourselves to our children. God intended for us to love them. Before we can do that, we must give our whole selves to Him.

My love for my children is not diminished; it is increased a thousand fold when I put Him first.

Prayer: Lord, help me to put you first so I can love others as you love them. Amen.

Count Your Blessings

*Praise the LORD, my soul;*
  *all my inmost being, praise his holy name.*
*² Praise the LORD, my soul,*
  *and forget not all his benefits—*
*³ who forgives all your sins*
  *and heals all your diseases,*
*⁴ who redeems your life from the pit*
  *and crowns you with love and compassion,*
*⁵ who satisfies your desires with good things*
  *so that your youth is renewed like the eagle's.* (Psalm 103: 1 – 5)

The message is clear: be truly grateful for all you have. Thank the Lord every day for what he has provided as well as what he has withheld. If you believe with all your heart that God only wants the best for you, you understand the truth of these words. We should be thankful just as much for what we don't get (trouble, worry, fear) as for what we do (hope, joy, eternal life).

Of course, sometimes we do get trouble. Be thankful then, too. While God only gives good things, we still encounter obstacles of pain, unhappiness, fear, or whatever is troubling to us. But God can turn those hurdles into bridges that lead to stronger resolve when we face them again – and we will face them again.

*For we know that all things work together for good to them that love the Lord and are called according to his purpose.* (Romans 8:28). All things – not just good things. It may take 20/20 hindsight to see troubles as blessings, but they are just the same. If we are faithful to his Word, God uses every experience for his glory. And he will reveal those good things in his own time. Some of my own experiences/trials have been pretty discouraging, and I admit it was hard to find any good result in them. But, if I am honest, I will also admit that God has used them in some amazing ways.

Take a few minutes and think about some discouragement you have faced, either by your own decision or someone else's. Has God worked through those experiences for the greater good? If you don't see it now, you will. He is truly the one who never lets a crisis go to waste; he will always use it for your good and his glory.

Remind yourself daily to count your blessings; name them one by one…

Prayer: Lord, help me to count my blessings and give you the praise and the glory. Amen.

## Look in the Mirror

*Anyone who listens to the Word but does not do what it says is like a man who looks at his face in a mirror and, after looking at himself, goes away and immediately forgets what he looks like.* (James 1:23 – 24)

Have you really looked in the mirror lately? For those of us who are getting older, it's not the treat it used to be. I am shocked sometimes when I see my reflection – the wrinkles, gray hair, loose skin where it used to be tight. I have to remind myself that these are merely physical traits. What happens if I look deeper, beyond the outer layer?

The scripture tells us to remember what we see when we look in the mirror. Are my deeds for the Lord imprinted on my face? Would others say they see my love of Christ in my actions? It is not enough to just read God's word; we must act in a way that brings glory to God and leaves no doubt that we are his children. Read on through verse 27. The instruction is very clear. You can't just be "religious." You have to live the Word!

I heard a radio ministry program that encouraged its listeners to take the 30/30 challenge to put God's word first every day for 30 days. Before you have coffee, shower, watch the morning news, or whatever your routine includes, spend thirty minutes with God. The recommendation was to start with Psalm 119, which the minister called the most inclusive instruction on God in God's word.

But, don't just read the words, meditate on them, seek God's direction from them, praise and worship with them. Stay on Psalm 119 for 30 days. Absorb it. Act on it. Memorize as much of it as you can.

Hold it in your heart.

At the end of this challenge, look again in the mirror. Be honest with yourself and determine if your life has changed as a result of meeting God in his word for those 30 days. (Check all that apply)

- ○ Less worldly
- ○ More generous
- ○ Less critical
- ○ More encouraging
- ○ Less judgmental
- ○ More forgiving
- ○ Less demanding
- ○ More loving

Stand before the mirror with your naked heart open to God. Who is looking back at you?

Prayer: Lord, I stand before you. Cleanse my heart and move me to change myself for you. Amen

Is God in Your life or is He in You?

*For it is no longer I who live, but Christ who lives in me. This life I live now I live by faith in the Son of the living God who loved me and gave his life for me.* (Galatians 2:20)

For so many of us, the first part of that question is all too true. We acknowledge God as real, but we're not quite sure who he is or what role he plays in our lives. I am fortunate that my conversion experience removed any doubt about that, but not everyone has such an experience. So, it is important to ask yourself the question, "Is God just in my life, or is God in me?"

How do you know?

Here are a few guideposts to determine if God is living in you through his Holy Spirit:

> **Prayer**: are your prayers structured to mostly plead with God for the things you want to happen, or do you listen quietly for his Spirit to speak to you?

> **Conviction**: do you feel convicted when you have said or done something you know is not bringing honor and glory to God? (Remember that feeling in the pit of your stomach that says, uh-oh?)

> **Service**: do you serve God and others with a joyful spirit, or do you serve only to get recognition or to take charge because you are the only one who can do it right?

> **Love**: do you love your neighbor as yourself, or do you just give lip service to it?

There are other signs, of course, but these four are a good start. It's a tough row to hoe, as my mother used to say. It takes a lot of determination, re-setting your compassion compass, dropping to your knees to ask forgiveness, and just starting each day with a renewed promise to seek God and let his Spirit guide your decisions.

We all make mistakes, say the wrong, or sometimes hurtful thing, but if God is living in you, you know what to do and you do it: Confess, ask for forgiveness and work to avoid making the same mistake again.

His Spirit will be there to help.

Prayer: Thank you, Lord, for sending your Holy Spirit to help me. Amen.

Paradox with a Purpose

*Be alert and of sober mind. Your enemy the devil prowls around like a roaring lion looking for someone to devour.* (1Peter 5:8)

*For the eyes of the LORD run to and fro throughout the whole earth, to give strong support to those whose heart is blameless toward him. You have done foolishly in this, for from now on you will have wars.* (2 Chronicles 16:9)

I heard these two verses on separate occasions this week, and when I heard the second one, it struck me that as I am driving in my car listening to the radio, there is a spiritual battle going on around me. It is a battle already won for me through my faith in Jesus Christ, but it is still there.

Think about it. The devil prowls around looking for someone to devour, and the Lord's eyes are running to and fro looking for those whom he can support. I don't know about you, but I would rather be sought by the Lord than the devil. I know there are many who don't believe in the devil, but God's Word makes it very clear that he is alive and well and hoping to cause pain and suffering wherever he can.

The Old Testament is jammed with examples: Job, Isaiah, Jonah, King David, Saul, and, of course, the original tempter in Genesis. The New Testament also supports the reality of Satan: Matthew, Mark and Luke all name Satan as the tempter of Jesus during his 40 days in the desert; Jesus warns his disciples and his followers about Satan; We also know that only Jesus has been able to resist Satan during his time on earth – we are all still vulnerable to his temptations.

But, let's concentrate for a moment on how the Lord is here to support those who love and honor him. We could spend an inordinate amount of time looking for the negative (Satan) while the Lord stands ready to support us if we only acknowledge him as our Savior. He offers a new strength to resist the devil. He is looking for "those whose hearts are blameless toward him.. And how are our hearts made blameless? Through the saving blood of Jesus Christ. We don't need to fear the power of Satan. We have an Advocate who protects us for eternity. That is not to say we won't have trouble. We will, and much of it will be of our own making. The good news is that, in the end, we will not be lost to Satan but will be glorified with Jesus Christ.

The last part of 2 Chronicles 16:9 is a cause and effect statement. You have done foolishly in this; i.e., you have not been obedient to Me. From now on you will have wars; i.e., you will have conflict – whether it is with others or within your own heart. We make choices; we live with the consequences. Those of us who have made our heartfelt commitment to Jesus will have his strength as we live through those consequences.

As for those who don't know him, well, you're on your own.

Prayer: Lord, speak to the hearts of those who don't yet know you, who are fighting the battle and help them to see your saving grace. Amen.

No Doubt

*We know that we have come to know him if we keep his commands. Whoever says, "I know him," but does not do what he commands is a liar, and the truth is not in that person. But if anyone obeys his word, love for God is truly made complete in them. This is how we know we are in him: Whoever claims to live in him must live as Jesus did.* (1 John 2: 3 – 6)

Once you have committed your life to Jesus Christ through your confession of sin and resolve to live for Him, you can be assured that you are saved and will spend eternity with Christ. While your salvation is secure, there is more to being a follower of Jesus. Read the scripture again. If you want to be a true Christian, you must live like one. "…live as Jesus did."

Does that mean you have to give up everything, find disciples and travel the world preaching? Not necessarily. Look at the big picture. Whom did Jesus serve? What was his attitude toward others? How did he express kindness, compassion and love? When did he pray? What did he teach by example?

If you can pattern your behavior after the answers to these questions, you will leave no doubt in the minds of others that you belong to Jesus Christ. We know that others are watching our actions; they are waiting for us to make a mistake so they can dismiss our witness and the claim of being Christian. I'm not saying you can't ever make a mistake in your Christian life, but I am saying you need to make the supreme effort not to stumble or cause someone else to stumble. (Romans 14:13)

So, let's talk about everyday situations. Be honest and record your first response to this situation and then consider it again with the eyes of the world watching:

- You get too much change at the Wal-Mart checkout.
- Your bill at the restaurant doesn't show the sodas you ordered… and drank.
- A co-worker is spreading gossip about your supervisor.
- Your daughter's friend is bragging about shoplifting a bracelet.
- You have the opportunity to buy an antique at a low price when you know the seller isn't aware of its real value.
- You witness a co-worker driving off after scraping against another car in the parking lot.
- You pay cash to your mechanic so he can avoid paying sales tax on the parts he sold you.

No big deal, right? None of these examples represent life and death. They aren't even things we encounter every day. But they illustrate being honest in the small things as an indicator of being honest with the big things as well.

And, it isn't just with material things; it's feelings, challenges, thoughts, and decisions. Everything we do and say indicates our true selves – honest or dishonest; little white lies or big whoppers, hidden or visible to all. Fight the urge to "just get by" and plunge into a commitment to be your best self for Jesus… and everyone else.

You will leave no doubt as to whom you serve.

Prayer: Lord, remind me in the little things that I am serving you and want to show others the right path. Amen.

Mining for Treasure

*My son, do not forget my teaching, but keep my commands in your heart, for they will prolong your life many years and bring you peace and prosperity.* (Proverbs 3: 1 – 2)

I'm sure my kids would tell you that I was a fount of wisdom and good teaching when they were growing up – ha ha. I don't know if they even remember some of the jewels I shared. I do know that my intentions were good; I wanted to set them on the right path – at least as much as I was able. I made sure they knew the sacrifice Christ had made for them and how much more fulfilling their lives would be if they chose to follow Him.

Here are some of the other teachings I shared:

- Be sure that your sin will find you out. You can't hide from God.
- Choose to be happy.
- Your brother/sister is the only other person in the world who shares your history. Family first.
- Save what you can; share what you can.
- Don't apologize for who you are.
- Work as if it all depends on you; pray as if it all depends on God.
- I'm your mother; no one on this earth will ever love you as much as I do. (I think they understand that one better now that they are both parents.)
- The most wonderful gift a father can give his children is to love their mother.

The fact is I only want the best for my children – just like you do. And like God does. We are his children, and he has wonderful plans for us. (Jeremiah 29: 11) He, too, has given us jewels to treasure in His Word – wisdom to share and put into action. Just reading Proverbs is enough to renew your strength for day to day living!

Remember, there are 31 chapters in Proverbs; if you read Chapter 1 on the first day and continue a chapter each day, you will finish in a month. So, start today, making notes of the most meaningful verses. You will be amazed at the gems you will discover.

Then share the wealth!

Prayer: Lord, help me to share my best with my children that they might trust in You also. Amen.

Jesus Loves Me

*For God so loved the world that He gave His only son so that whoever believes in him may not perish but have eternal life.* (John 3:16)

Such a simple truth. Why are we so quick to reject it? I became a Christian 35 years ago, and since that time I have heard every reason you can think of to explain away the truth of this statement. Here are a few:

- Well, I don't really believe in the Bible. I still think somebody just made that stuff up.
- It's fine for you, but it doesn't really work for me.
- Too simple; I need something more.
- Are you still leaning on that crutch? Get over it. You live; you die. That's it.
- I'm still on the fence; can't quite make up my mind.

Any of these statements sound familiar? Here are a few ideas on how to prepare to answer these doubts if you have the opportunity.

First, I would recommend "Seven Reasons Why You can Trust the Bible," by Erwin Lutzer. Dr. Lutzer is the senior pastor at Moody Bible Church in Chicago. Reading his book has armed me with the information I need to dispel concerns about the Bible's truth. He offers his arguments in such a logical and supportable way that I truly feel more confident in sharing its truth.

I had a friend who used the "too simple" response to my attempts to share the Gospel with her. She said she needed something on a higher intellectual plane to satisfy her longing for peace in her heart. I reminded her that the message is simple on purpose. The Lord would never make His salvation message something that only a few could decipher and act upon. He offers his love and forgiveness to

ALL. "Because ALL have sinned and fall short of the glory of God." (Romans 3:23 – 24). If we are all sinners then we also are all given the choice of repentance and salvation.

Another friend claimed to "still be on the fence" during a discussion about salvation. I put my arm gently around his shoulders and said, "Darlin' there is no fence. You're in or you're out, and right now, you're out." That may sound blunt, but sometimes you have to be; eternity is a very, very long time. I also asked him again if he would like to accept Jesus as Lord and Savior, but he just smiled and walked away.

I am sad to say that neither of these friends has made a commitment to Jesus Christ. They are still searching, but they won't find anything more satisfying or complete than a love for Jesus Christ. He is waiting with open arms for them and anyone else who is willing to admit a need for his love and forgiveness.

Where do you stand? Answer His call to your heart.

It's as simple as that.

Prayer: Lord, I know I am a sinner. I need and want your forgiveness. Please come into my heart. Amen.